may you be inspired [to nurture?] yourself & thrive! sending you peace, love and gratitude, Kelley ♡

The Art of Self-Nurturing

A FIELD GUIDE TO LIVING WITH MORE PEACE, JOY, & MEANING

KELLEY GRIMES, MSW

INSPIRED LIVING PUBLISHING, LLC.
www.InspiredLivingPublishing.com

A SUPPORTIVE GIFT FROM MY HEART TO YOURS!

THE **Self-Nurturing** STARTER KIT

YOUR SUPPORTIVE STARTER KIT INCLUDES:

- The Arrival Technique Guided Meditation *(mp3)*
- Permission to Nurture Yourself Audio Guide *(mp3)*
- Beautiful printable Self-Nurturing Affirmations Poster *(PDF)*
- Soothing printable Self-Nurturing Breathe Cards *(PDF)*
- Printable Self-Nurturing Permission Slip *(PDF)*

SAY YES TO YOURSELF AND DOWNLOAD YOUR SELF-NURTURING STARTER KIT TODAY AT:

www.ArtofSelfNurturingBook.com/starterkit

Published by Inspired Living Publishing, LLC.
P.O. Box 1149, Lakeville, MA 02347

ISBN-13: 978-1-7327425-3-6

Library of Congress Control Number: 2020915274

www.InspiredLivingPublishing.com
(508) 265-7929

Cover and Layout Design: Rachel Dunham www.YourBrandTherapy.com

Layout: Patricia Creedon www.PatCreedonDesign.com

Editor: Deborah Kevin www.DeborahKevin.com

Printed in the United States.

To Fiona and Zoey,

my beloved daughters who
have taught me how important
it is to nurture myself and
share these lessons with
the world. I love you both so
incredibly much and am deeply
grateful for all the love and
light you bring to my life and
to the world!

"**The Art of** Self-Nurturing is a thought-provoking, heartfelt, and inspirational book, providing the reader clear insights on the need to prioritize our wellbeing. Kelley Grimes has written a practical guidebook on how to self-nurture with tangible tools and foundational practices. I appreciate how well thought out and laid out this book is, especially now. With everything going on in the world, I cannot think of a better guidebook to come out that can teach people how to nourish themselves from the inside out, and how to integrate these practices into our daily lives. Everyone needs to read this book."

-Lisa Rueff
Founder and Chief Heart Warrior of Collective Hearts

"WOW! **The Art of** Self-Nurturing is a must-read! Congratulations and a heartfelt thank you to Kelley for this joyful compilation of helpful, tangible and inspiring ideas and ways to bring more self-nurturing to ourselves, thus giving us the ability to bring more joy to others. This is LOVE in a book. It's exactly what the world needs more of now!"

-Wendy Urushima-Conn
President & CEO Epilepsy Foundation of San Diego County

"Like any good field guide, **The Art of** *Self-Nurturing* is an easy to use resource. This guide helps you identify and navigate the journey toward a better relationship with yourself. Kelley's passion is contagious! Her field guide provides handholds to start where you are, and touchstones for further growth."

–Katia Hansen
President & CEO of UURISE

"Kelley Grimes is an amazing teacher and role model for negotiating the delicate balance between self-nurturing while generously showing up in passionate care for others. Her authenticity is infectious. Read **The Art of** *Self-Nurturing*. Leverage her journey. Apply her teachings."

–Lisane Basquiat
Life Strategist

"Kelley's words resonate with me deeply as I am a beginner on this self-nurturing journey. For too long, as a wife, mother, daughter, and corporate climber, I put myself at the bottom of my priority list. I'm excited about Kelley's book, **The Art of** *Self-Nurturing*, as I feel it's written exactly right. Not only does Kelley's experience and expertise shine through her words but also her heart. This will be a great resource on the journey to be better at self-nurturing, something needed to attain the best life I want to live."

–Tanya Thompson
Director of Global Product Acquisition Hasbro Gaming and Self-Nurturing student.

"Kelley Grimes has given us an important gift–permission to care for ourselves. As an activist, I see people becoming exhausted doing justice work in these unsettling times. Kelley artfully guides us into the revolutionary act of nurturing ourselves so that we may, in turn, nurture and transform the world."

–Rev. Dr. Beth Johnson
Minister, Activist, Public Theologian

PRAISE FOR The Art of Self-Nurturing

"In her powerful new book, **The Art of Self-Nurturing**, Kelley Grimes, MSW shows you how to cultivate a life of self-love and compassion by letting go of living from obligation and overwhelm through her self-nurturing program. She empowers you to be the artist of your life by providing inspiration, examples, and self-nurturing practices to support you on your spiritual journey. Kelley reminds you that the most important relationship you have is with yourself---that you alone have the power within you to create a purposeful, happy, and joy-filled life. A must-read for anyone who wants to know how to nurture and take precious care of themselves."

–Dr. Debra L. Reble
Intuitive Psychologist, Transformational Coach, and Best-Selling Author

"Kelley has written an important and timely wake-up call to anyone who thinks self-nurturing is optional, or out of reach. She shows readers that not only is self-nurturing necessary, but it's also totally possible through small, simple practices that add up over time to joy."

–Mia Moran
Bestselling Author and Productivity Coach

"Kelley Grimes lights the way to nourish and nurture your most enlivened, creative, and empowered self. **The Art of Self-Nurturing** is a life-changing book. You don't want to miss it!"

–Terry Laszlo-Gopadze
Marriage and Family Therapist and Editor of "The Spirit of a Woman: Stories to Empower and Inspire"

"As women, we're so often juggling multiple priorities, nurturing everyone and everything around us, except for ourselves. In **The Art of Self-Nurturing**, Kelley Grimes lovingly guides women on a journey of self-discovery, self-compassion, and self-nurturing. She offers wonderful, easy to implement strategies we can practice each day to ensure that we treat ourselves with the same importance we treat others. Kelley shows us how to stay refreshed, recharged, and inspired to be our best selves."

–Dr. Colleen Georges
Author of the Award-Winning book, RESCRIPT the Story You're Telling Yourself

The Art of Self-Nurturing

"Kelley Grimes has cultivated a way of life that is resplendent and devoted even as she is in service through her work, community, and family. What an honor she has gifted us with this extraordinary field guide, based on her decades of wisdom and practice, inviting us to cultivate an abundant devotion to ourselves. With reflective prompts, rich stories, and practical examples, this guide will be a book that open-hearted givers return to again and again. Thank you, Kelley, for showing us the way!"

–Shannon Weber, MSW
Author, Show Up Hard: A Road Map for Helpers In Crisis

"**The Art of Self-Nurturing** is a precious gem that every woman will treasure. So many useful tools, tips, and thought-provoking questions. Kelley Grimes speaks to all women in this must-have guide to self-love and joyful living! Thank you for this amazing gift!"

–Kris Groth
Spiritual Mentor, Energy Healer, Archangel Life Coach & Bestselling Author

"Kelley Grimes, MSW, has trained hundreds of non-profit professionals in San Diego County on self-nurturing. I am so glad she will be able to help even more people with this wonderful book. The impactful lessons you will learn in **The Art of Self-Nurturing** will steer you towards a more meaningful and peaceful life."

–Marylynn McCorkle
Collaboration Coordinator for the Alliance for Regional Solutions

"You will cry tears of joy as you learn to release the baggage of self-improvement to-do lists! Kelley Grimes' **The Art of Self-Nurturing** takes you on a journey of sacred self-reflection in which you leave overwhelm and resentment behind and discover your peace-filled authentic self."

–Kathleen Gubitosi, MA
Voice Strategist and Feminine Power Guide

"A timely and impactful guide for women that reveals the connection of how our interpretation of our value and worth can be healed and transformed through the art of self-nurturing. There has never been a greater need for self-nurturing, and Kelley's **The Art of** *Self-Nurturing* guides us toward the magic that prioritizing ourselves brings."

–Colleen Elaine
RTT Therapist & Board Certified Hypnotherapist

"Kelley's voice and teachings are crucial for every living being; she lives her message of self-nurturing and, as a result, radiates true, authentic love in all that she does. It is a great truth that the kindness we extend to others can only be a reflection of the kindness that we give ourselves. The old image of the stressed-out, over-taxed, over-booked "cool" has got to go...for the sake of ourselves and the planet. Kelley's advice deeply resonates and is imperative as a foundation for our lives."

–Kelly Mellos
Fine Artist, Author, and Speaker

"Kelley Grimes has birthed a brilliant book showing women how to empower themselves through the art of self-nurturing. This field guide gives you all the practices you need and how to integrate them into your life for optimal effect. It's time to put down your "to-do" list and start embracing this "for me" guide. You are so worth it!"

–Mal Duane
Transformational Life Coach & Bestselling Author of Broken Open and Alpha Chick

"There is no single relationship more important than the one we have with ourselves. Kelley Grimes walks you through practical steps on how to nurture and love yourself, equipping the reader to move from exhaustion and burnout to joy and peace."

–Shannon Wills
Social Worker and Advocate

"Kelley Grimes truly is an Artist of Self-Love. It has taken me over forty years to discover, take care of, and know the real me before I can truly and purely serve others. **The Art of** *Self-Nurturing* opens the door to an entirely new era of love for ourselves so that we may unwrap this blessing for others."

–Helice "Grandma Sparky" Bridges,
Founder Blue Ribbons Worldwide, The First Lady of Acknowledgment, TEDx Presenter, best-selling author, mentor, trainer, and entertainer

"I truly hope you give yourself "permission" to read **The Art-of** *Self-Nurturing* and implement these practices into your life. I work with hundreds of female entrepreneurs who struggle with balance, boundaries, and self-compassion. I love how Kelley frames this process for every aspect of our lives–such as aging, our bodies, and our families. These routine practices can help women grow their businesses and expand the impact of their leadership. I've attended some of Kelley's events, and she really walks the talk. She is authentic, loving, supportive, and has a very peaceful presence."

–Felena Hanson,
Founder of Hera Hub, Workspace for Women

"Kelley Grimes has an amazing way about her. I'm aware of it each time we meet, and that's been 15 years in the making. Empathy, positivity, equality, justice, peace, and compassion – these are the very first six descriptors that come to mind when I think of Kelley. I think she's been able to make a significant impact in the lives of those fortunate enough to interact with her, both professionally and personally."

–Maggie Matthews,
Senior Vice President Licensing at the OP

"I can't think of a more opportune time in our history to inspire self-care and healing. To truly show up for others, we have to first show up for ourselves. We have to remember change begins with ourselves; this is an inside job. **The Art of** *Self-Nurturing* can be the guide we are all so hungry for on how to integrate the practice of loving ourselves daily to help transform ourselves and the world."

> **—Tasreen Khamisa,**
> *Executive Director, Tariq Khamisa Foundation*

In **The Art of** *Self-Nurturing*, Kelley Grimes draws an essential distinction between self-nurturing and the popular definition of self-care. Deciding and committing to nurture ourselves as a life choice sends a potent message internally and to others that we love and respect ourselves. True self-nurturing infuses all areas of our lives, filling every nook and cranny with more clarity, joy, peace, love, meaning, and belonging. It begins with belonging to ourselves. **The Art of** *Self-Nurturing* teaches how."

> **—Anne Wade,**
> *Teacher, Coach, and Storyworker*

"She's done it again and reminded me to love myself like I would a treasured friend. I've watched Kelley craft this approach for more than twenty-five years, for herself for others, for humanity. It's not easy centering ourselves. I am a Black woman, a mama, a leader, and if I don't love me like the gift I am...will my kids know love? Can I push for justice and be violent or disregard the beauty that is me? No. The answer is no.

> **—Kelly E. Perez,**
> *CEO/founder KindColorado & Co-ED of the Cannabis Impact Fund*

Table of Contents

Foreword

How many of us truly take time to self-nurture? Do we even know what that means? This term, 'self-nurture' may be new to you; however, it is critical today as more people are feeling anxious, stressed out, and concerned for their well-being. Self-nurturing can be the key to give you the insight and awareness to choose how you respond to life rather than to be at its mercy. In a world that seems very much out of control, the idea of taking control of your life and not being a victim to circumstances is essential.

Kelley Grimes has written a beautiful guide that can be your pathway to healing and wholeness. What you'll find here are powerful, life-changing ideas. How do I know this? I've seen them work for countless women overcoming some of life's toughest challenges. These challenges include domestic violence, homelessness, addiction, and disabling mental and physical health problems. One thing that many of these women have in common is they lost trust in themselves and had almost given up on life. For many who made mistakes, didn't speak up, or made poor choices, life turned out very different than they hoped or imagined. They experienced a downward spiral of guilt, shame, and regret, which led to a diminished belief in themselves. Thoughts and words of unworthiness and powerlessness became self-fulfilling prophecies.

But life doesn't have to be that way for any of us, no matter what happened in the past. Change and transformation are possible, especially when we learn new ways of thinking, speaking, and caring for ourselves. We have the power to change and create a new story and a new future. In fact, we are the only ones who can.

I first met Kelley in 2013 when I was looking to add to our team at Leap to Success. Leap to Success empowers women and helps them heal, grow, and recover from life challenges and trauma. Kelley appeared at the perfect moment with the perfect credentials and an abundance of passion and zeal for empowering women. She had everything I was looking for and more! What makes Kelley so successful in helping people is her tool chest of teachings that include self-nurturing as the foundation.

Kelley sparkles with infectious enthusiasm and joy. She enters any room with a huge smile and warmth that everyone can feel. She is also a world-class hugger. You'd never know from meeting her that she had experienced grief and trauma for many years as she dealt with her daughter Fiona's life-threatening health challenges. The lessons of self-nurturing that Kelley shares have been her personal path to healing and transformation. These powerful tools are right here in your hands and available to you now.

You might be afraid that self-nurturing is just another new thing to tackle or add to your already lengthy to-do list, but don't be concerned, here's how Kelley explains it, "I believe self-nurturing is an art form. The practice is not about being perfect or completing another thing on your "to-do" list, but rather nurturing a relationship with yourself. It is about recognizing what is nurturing in any given moment and allowing your practice to evolve accordingly."

We all know a woman, and might even be one, who puts everyone ahead of herself to the point of exhaustion and overwhelm. If you were in that situation and came to see Kelley with eyes full of tears feeling burned out, imagine hearing her gently ask, 'What would you tell your best friend if she was feeling the way you are right now?' That one simple question could help you shift to a more compassionate and self-nurturing mode. It's often easier to see how we care for those we love than how we treat and care for ourselves.

By holding this book in your hands, you are poised to start a journey of self-discovery. As with any travel, it's important to be prepared. Luckily, preparation is easy. This journey just takes your willingness and openness to try some new ideas. You have an expert guide ready to gently assist you in finding your way home where all is safe and well. There you're next to a fire that is warm and cozy, and you are sitting with your best friend. What you may be startled to find is that your best friend is someone extraordinarily special... because she is you.

Enjoy your journey!

Dana Bristol-Smith
Founder & Executive Director, Leap to Success
www.LeaptoSuccess.org

Introduction + Welcome

Welcome to *The Art of Self-Nurturing*, your field guide to living with more peace, joy, and meaning! Thank you so much for joining me on this journey! I want to begin by acknowledging you for picking up this book. I know how hard it is when you are feeling overwhelmed and exhausted to do one more thing. I have been where you are wishing life would be different but not knowing how. I am honored to share my lessons and best self-nurturing practices with you so you can begin transforming your life today.

My intention for this book is to empower you to become the artist of your own life. Rather than living from obligation and overwhelm, I hope that you will learn to cultivate a life filled with self-compassion and self-love. What I have learned from countless clients and my own experience is that the more we nurture ourselves, the more we acknowledge our value and worth. The more we recognize our value and worth, the more we prioritize nurturing ourselves. This process creates a beautiful self-supporting cycle that continually reminds us of the power and importance of nurturing ourselves!

This field guide is designed to make your journey easier and to support you by breaking down the process into three parts: The Foundation of Self-Nurturing, Cultivating a Self-Nurturing Practice, and Integrating Self-Nurturing Practices into Your Life. Each section is broken into chapters and will provide inspiration, best practices, examples, reflective questions, and self-nurturing practices. You can read the book through to the end and then use it for on-going support. The field guide offers you hundreds of self-nurturing practices that you can try over time and return to as you build your practice and incorporate more strategies. Cultivating a self-nurturing practice is an evolving process that benefits us most when we integrate it into our lives.

I believe self-nurturing is an art form. The practice is not about being perfect or completing another thing on your "to-do" list, but rather nurturing a relationship with yourself. It is about recognizing what is nurturing in any given moment and allowing your practice to evolve accordingly. Self-nurturing embraces your individual preferences, provides opportunities to learn about yourself, and express your authenticity and creativity. The more we nurture ourselves, the more we know ourselves allowing us to reveal more of who we are in the world. Self-nurturing can be an individual or shared experience and helps us understand more about ourselves and the world around us, just like art. This journey is about the process, not a final product, and will unfold in beautiful and inspiring ways.

I want to encourage you to invite in a spirit of curiosity and non-judgment as you begin this process and cultivate it throughout the journey. Curiosity and non-judgment are profoundly nurturing and naturally open our hearts and minds to make learning easier. As you read this book, please permit yourself to be present, recognizing that you are investing in yourself. Please let go of the thought that these self-nurturing practices are another thing to add to your "to-do" list. Instead, bring the spirit of nurturing to the process of reading. Woven throughout this book are reminders that you matter, you are loved, you are important, and you deserve to give to yourself the love and kindness that you spread in the world. With each act of self-nurturing, you will remember these sacred truths!

You are now on the adventure of a lifetime, nurturing the most important relationship you will ever have–the relationship with yourself! I have come to understand that to be of greatest service in the world and be sustainable in our giving, we must come from a filled-up place where we can nurture peace from the inside out. When we understand this powerful truth, nurturing ourselves then becomes essential to nurturing others. Imagine how different your life will be when your cup is so full you can give from the overflow in your saucer? Imagine the positive impact you will have in the world. Imagine how much more peace, joy, and meaning you will experience.

I am thrilled that we are embarking on this adventure together, and I am here to support you the whole way! If you are ready to begin, let's pause for a moment and take a deep breath. Savor this breath, your constant companion, and the best way to connect with yourself in any given moment. Allow your next exhale to be the permission you need to release anything that is not serving you in this moment. Now set an intention for your self-nurturing journey, such as courage, love, and/or gratitude. Keep a journal handy to record your wisdom and insights. My intention for this book is that my words empower all who read them, embody love, compassion, and joy, and nurture healing and positive change in the world with ease and grace. Let's begin!

My Journey + Lessons

> "Joy does not simply happen to us.
> We have to choose joy and keep
> choosing it every day."
>
> -Henri J.M. Nouwen

You may be wondering how I came to write a book on self-nurturing. There were times in my life that it would have been much more likely for me to write a book on nurturing others than on nurturing myself. I learned to be an expert in nurturing others, as I imagine you have too–as a mother, daughter, wife, sister, counselor, volunteer, mentor, and friend. However, I was unskilled at nurturing myself. As my challenges transformed into possibilities, I learned powerful life lessons about the need for self-nurturing. I am deeply grateful for the wisdom and insights I have gained as a result.

Whenever I learn something transformative, I always want to share this wisdom with others. I have been teaching the lessons you will find in this book to my individual clients, couples, families, in workshops, retreats, and keynote speeches for over a decade. It has been my dream to write a book to share these transformational tools of self-nurturing with more people.

One of the best teachers I have had on my self-nurturing journey has been my oldest daughter, Fiona. When Fiona was two years-old, she had her first epileptic seizure at daycare, which was not properly assessed. By the time my husband arrived to take her to the doctor, he realized something was terribly wrong and took her immediately to the emergency room. When I arrived at the ER, I felt the anxiety and fear of the staff as they quickly ushered me into her room. What I saw next left an indelible mark on my heart and mind—my tiny daughter, close to death, seizing on the table. By the time they stopped her seizure, it had lasted fifty-five minutes, and my sweet girl had nearly died.

This formative experience as a new parent guided me to live in fear for my daughter's safety and quickly learn how to predict her needs and care for them. I became an expert in nurturing her and everyone around me as it gave me purpose and meaning in a world that often felt out of control. One of the unique characteristics of epilepsy is that seizures are unpredictable and so I lived in constant crisis management mode, needing to be available at any moment to support Fiona regardless of where I was. Living with this high level of stress exhausted me, and the burden of responsibility became overwhelming.

And, as life often offers us, there were many more challenges to overcome. Not long after Fiona was diagnosed with epilepsy, I became pregnant with my daughter, Zoey. Six months into my pregnancy, my grandmother and father died within two weeks of each other. I experienced pre-term labor, was hospitalized, and placed on bed rest for the remainder of my pregnancy. After Zoey was born, she had health challenges that resulted in multiple hospitalizations.

Over time Fiona's seizures increased in frequency, and when she was eight years old, she started having migraines that lasted four days after each seizure. I supported Fiona with all the impacts of her seizures: academic, social, emotional, and medical, and constantly advocated for her needs.

I continued to work as a counselor during this time, as well as for different non-profit organizations including the Epilepsy Foundation. As a result, I was drowning in responsibility, overwhelm, and despair and was desperate for my life to be different.

On a walk one evening, I thought to myself, it would be easier to step in front of the next passing car than it would be to continue living this way. Fortunately, I asked myself, what would be the antidote to feeling this despair and hopelessness? And the response was joy! I felt so grateful for this insight and quickly focused my energy on finding ways to bring joy into my life. Those finely honed research skills I developed from years of seeking solutions to Fiona's health challenges allowed me to cultivate joy in my life by meditating, practicing daily gratitude, and spending time in nature. I played games with my family and reminded myself that in each moment, all was well. I noticed a shift immediately and recognized what a difference it made to be consistent with these new practices. Falling back into caring for others before caring for myself was all too easy, so understanding this as a daily practice was essential.

11

Over time, I established an empowering self-nurturing practice, which had an incredibly positive impact on my life, my family's lives, and my clients' lives. In really caring for myself, I was better able to care for those around me, improving my ability to be truly present with others, compassionate, patient, understanding, loving, and give from a full heart. My exhaustion and overwhelm eased and then faded, and I discovered through my daily self-nurturing practice that I was kinder and more loving to myself.

The results of these shifts revolutionized my life and the lives of my clients. In this field guide, I'll share some of their inspiring stories with you and the lessons I have learned on this journey of discovery and self-nurturing. If you are feeling overwhelmed and exhausted right now, you are not alone. There is hope, and we can make new choices. We can choose joy and keep choosing it every day.

How To Use This Field Guide

"The only journey is the one within.

-Rainer Maria Rilke

The gift of a field guide is that it is a resource you can return to over and over again. As you begin your self-nurturing journey, invite in a spirit of curiosity and adventure. Each chapter of this guide includes a treasure trove to explore, including: a quote for inspiration, best practices for applying the lessons, examples of other brave travelers, reflective questions to learn more about yourself, and a variety of self-nurturing practices to try. In some chapters, I have included a touchstone symbol to remind you to nurture yourself as well as affirmations to encourage you.

In the third section of the book, Integrating Self-Nurturing Practices into Your Life, you will find twenty-two brief chapters addressing specific opportunities to nurture yourself. There is an alphabetized index in the Table of Contents to help you locate these practices quickly.

As you read this book, put into practice what resonates with you, knowing that there is no need to put everything you learn into action. The foundation of self-nurturing is getting to know yourself, so start at a pace that reflects where you are right now in your life. If you are completely overwhelmed, permit yourself to start slowly. If you have the energy for significant changes, add more practices into your day. Learning to nurture yourself and prioritize time to care for yourself is part of the self-nurturing journey, so commit to giving yourself grace in the process. Using a journal to answer the reflective questions throughout the book will be a supportive and nurturing way to document your journey, progress, and evolving practice.

It is natural as we make changes in our lives to begin enthusiastically, and as time passes, fall back into our old ways. If this happens to you, I invite you to respond to yourself with compassion and kindness. Then return to this book. Open it to where you left off and begin again. Or open the book to a random page and see what wisdom is meant for you at that moment. Give yourself permission from the start to return to the practice. As you begin this process, write yourself a permission slip stating, "I give myself permission to be kind and loving to myself as I learn how to nurture myself." When we let go of perfectionism and instead choose what could nurture us in this moment, we liberate ourselves from "shoulds" and obligation and open to the magic unfolding in front of us.

Learning to prioritize yourself will be the most transformational gift you can give yourself, so be gentle in the process and return to this field guide as often as you need to. I hope that you will see this book as a resource and guide on your journey of creating a more loving and kind relationship with yourself. As you embrace the art of self-nurturing, you will learn so much about yourself, and each self-nurturing choice will remind you of your inherent worth and value. This field guide lays out steps for you to build upon, starting with the foundations of self-nurturing, then teaches you how to cultivate a self-nurturing practice, and finally how to integrate self-nurturing practices into your life. Bring an intention of nurturing to the process, and let's dive in!

PART ONE

Foundations of Self Nurturing

What is Self-Nurturing?

"For most of us, the word nurture from the Latin "nutritus" for "nourish," conjures up images of taking care of others with lovingly prepared food, emotional support, protective warmth, practical help, and wise teachings. In self-nurture, we offer ourselves these same gifts, and more, as daily practice."

-Alice Domar

Self-nurturing is all about how we treat ourselves. It is the practice of treating ourselves like we would a cherished friend, listening to our feelings and needs, and prioritizing ourselves in our lives. To nurture ourselves is to lovingly care for ourselves in all areas of our lives, allowing us to truly know ourselves, express our authentic truth, and protect ourselves when necessary. Self-nurturing is the ultimate empowerment strategy that offers us the transformational gift of being loving and kind to ourselves on this journey of life.

And indeed, the practice of self-nurturing is foundational to our health and happiness. Our ability to nurture ourselves impacts all areas of our lives, whether we are conscious of this or not, including our self-worth, our families, our careers, our health, our purpose, and every relationship we have. As you learn to nurture yourself, every area of your life will transform, and you will begin living with more peace, joy, and meaning.

You may have heard the wisdom that we teach other people how to treat us. My experience validates this thinking. Committing to nurture ourselves consistently sends a powerful message to the world that we love and respect ourselves. Our value and worth are the foundation of self-nurturing, reinforced with our every action. The greatest gifts of self-nurturing are that the more you nurture yourself, the more you love and value yourself. The more you love and appreciate yourself, the more you prioritize nurturing yourself, creating a beautiful self-sustaining cycle.

Understanding this truth allows us to minimize feeling guilty or selfish when we nurture ourselves because we recognize that it is the only path to sustainable giving. When we begin including ourselves when making decisions and do not give more of ourselves than we have to give, we can give generously. Imagine again being so filled up that you give from the overflow of your cup rather than your last drops.

You will notice that I use the term self-nurturing rather than self-care. I see self-nurturing as the expanded, more comprehensive version of self-care. Self-nurturing is not just about the self-care activities, but rather about the relation-ship we are developing with ourselves and how we engage in an activity. I have heard from many clients that sometimes self-care can feel like another "to do" on their overflowing lists. There is an experience of "I should do this" or "I should do that". Instead, self-nurturing is about the way we treat and care for ourselves. The motivation around self-nur-turing comes from within and carries with it the energy of choice rather than an obligation. As a result, any activity can be self-nurturing when you bring that intention to it.

I define self-nurturing as the act of deeply caring for your-self by nourishing, cherishing, and encouraging your own growth and potential. There are so many ways we can nour-ish, cherish, and encourage our growth and potential that you will find within these pages. If you are used to using the term self-care, that is fine, but I encourage you to try on self-nurturing and see if it feels different and more expan-sive. My hope for you is that you will bring this new spirit of nurturing to your relationship with yourself and notice the difference it makes.

Reflective
Questions

1.

HOW DO YOU NOURISH YOURSELF?

2.

HOW DO YOU CHERISH YOURSELF?

3.

**HOW DO YOU ENCOURAGE YOUR OWN GROWTH
AND POTENTIAL?**

Why Self-Nurture?

"Most importantly, be gentle with yourself. You can't hate yourself into change. You can't shame yourself into change. It just doesn't work. The one way change can happen is if you can love yourself as you are, and then, from that place of love, you can muster up the faith and courage you'll need in order to do what must be done."

-Tosha Silver

*I*f we understand the concept of putting on our own oxygen mask before helping others, then why is it so hard to put this wisdom into action? The answer lies with the false belief, so many women hold that to have value, we must take care of other people. Traditionally women were socialized to nurture others and attached their value and worth to this role. Over time more roles were added to our expectations of women, including working outside the home, volunteering in the community, holding leadership roles of different kinds, and being the best mother, daughter, partner, and friend that they can be. The expectation that women should be everything to everyone results in women feeling that they never measure up. I have often heard women say that there must be something wrong with them that they cannot meet these unattainable standards. These unrealistic expectations fuel the cycle of giving more and more, which leads to more exhaustion, overwhelm, and resentment and fuels women feeling guilty or selfish taking time for themselves.

This unhealthy cycle leads many women to feel like they are living life on a hamster wheel, struggling to get all the things done they need to, and feeling little joy or meaning as a result. Trying to meet unrealistic expectations leaves women chronically overwhelmed, exhausted, and stressed, which negatively impacts their health, mental health, and relationships. Our "to-do" lists overflow with tasks, and when we think about caring for ourselves, it can often feel like another responsibility to add to our lists. Many women recognize that this is no way to live, but don't know where to even begin to break the cycle.

I believe that the time of the self-sacrificing women is over. In truth, self-sacrificing women can be impatient, frustrated, and resentful due to their overwhelm and exhaustion. They are not able to be fully present with anyone. We have held that version of the ideal woman for too long, and it is time to transform it, one empowered, self-nurturing woman at a time. The antidote for the overwhelmed and exhausted woman is self-nurturing. I have found that self-nurturing is the only way to connect to the inherent worth within each of us. It is the way out of exhaustion and overwhelm into peace, joy, and meaning.

And while we are transforming the world, let's not leave men out. I have worked with men in my counseling practice who have also been trapped in this cycle of unrealistic expectations, giving to everyone in their lives, leaving them exhausted and overwhelmed. These men believed they must provide to have value and worth and felt guilty taking time to nurture and care for themselves. They usually had limited ways of understanding how to nurture themselves, like exercise, for example, and if they got injured, they could think of no other options.

In my practice and life, I have found self-nurturing to be the answer to so many challenges. It is the way out of exhaustion and overwhelm and into health and wellness. It is the light that can transform the darkness of unrealistic expectations and the hope for humanity to live with more love and compassion in the world. It is the way out of a scarcity mindset and into an abundance mindset, where there is so much more possibility. Self-nurturing opens us to more creativity, awareness, insight, and wisdom than we knew was possible. It gives us direct access to our truth and intuition. I have witnessed remarkable healing and empowerment when clients have understood the power of self-nurturing. Time after time, clients have identified self-nurturing as the key that transformed their lives. I am deeply grateful to have experienced that personally and hope you will too!

Reflective
Questions

1.

WHAT STOPS YOU FROM NURTURING YOURSELF?

2.

WHAT EXPECTATIONS DO YOU HAVE OF YOURSELF
WHEN IT COMES TO GIVING TO OTHERS?

3.

WHEN DO YOU FEEL GUILTY OR SELFISH WHEN
TAKING TIME FOR YOURSELF?

4.

HOW COULD NURTURING YOURSELF TRANSFORM
YOUR LIFE?

The Benefits of Self-Nurturing

"With a daily ritual of self-care, an inner worthiness begins to blossom. Once it does, you will find the courage to act in ways that are self-expressive and self-protective. You will start caring for each part of yourself with a fierce and tender concern."

~Alice D. Domar and Henry Dreher

I love this quote by Alice Domar and Henry Dreher because it highlights the ultimate benefit of self-nurturing–allowing your inner worthiness to blossom. Indeed, when we connect to our value and worth, we can more easily care for ourselves with a fierce and tender concern. Spending time exploring the benefits of self-nurturing will motivate you to commit to nurturing yourself. When you do, the benefits of self-nurturing will ripple out into every area of your life positively impacting you as an individual, family, community, and society.

When we consistently nurture ourselves, we feel less stress, overwhelm, exhaustion, and resentment, and more peace, joy, clarity, awareness, insight, energy, confidence, and meaning in our lives. Our ability to be generous, compassionate, loving, creative, kind, resilient, and grateful is increased by every act of self-nurturing. The more filled up we are, the easier it is to speak our truth and show up authentically with an open heart in the world. When we nurture ourselves regularly, we naturally come from an abundance mindset, allowing love to be our guide when making decisions. Nurturing ourselves reinforces the understanding that we must be loving and kind to ourselves in order to be genuinely loving and kind to others. As Thich Nhat Hanh reminds us, "Love is the capacity to take care, to protect, to nourish. If you are not capable of generating that kind of energy toward yourself–if you are not capable of taking care of yourself, of nourishing yourself, of protecting yourself–it is very difficult to take care of another person."

Nurturing ourselves also improves our overall health and wellness. When we cultivate a self-nurturing practice, we learn to listen consistently and compassionately to our feelings, our bodies, and our needs. Listening to ourselves is crucial to making healthy decisions and setting healthy boundaries. When cultivating a nurturing relationship with ourselves, we prioritize our needs and transform our habit of self-neglect.

30

A beautiful example of this comes from one of my early clients who joyfully shared her revolutionary self-nurturing practice: going to the bathroom when she needed to without her children. That simple act of listening to her basic human need was a concrete way to prioritize her needs that positively impacted many other areas of her life. Nurturing a relationship with ourselves means that we include our needs and feelings as part of the equation and decision-making process. As we learn to care for each part of ourselves with a fierce and tender concern, our health naturally improves, as does our overall sense of wellbeing. Instead of getting terribly sick before we slow down, we can choose to rest when we first feel a tingling in our throat. Learning to listen to our bodies and make nurturing choices is how we demonstrate our love and care for ourselves and is a powerful benefit of self-nurturing.

Regularly nurturing ourselves also supports us in feeling less stressed, more resilient, and more connected to ourselves and our families. How we treat ourselves informs others how to treat us and models healthy boundaries to those around us. When we choose to treat ourselves with kindness and compassion, we teach others by our example, and the ripple effects are endless. I truly believe that self-nurturing is at the root of healthy living for ourselves, our families, our communities, and society. If you want to nurture peace in the world, begin with nurturing peace within yourself. Our commitment to nurturing ourselves is the way to make the world a little kinder. We start by being kinder to ourselves and spreading that love and kindness in the world. The benefits of self-nurturing are endless and continue to unfold as you cultivate your self-nurturing practice.

Reflective
Questions

1.

WHAT BENEFITS ARE YOU MOST LOOKING
FORWARD TO EXPERIENCING AS YOU LEARN TO
NURTURE YOURSELF?

2.

WHAT WOULD IT LOOK LIKE TO CARE FOR
YOURSELF WITH A FIERCE AND TENDER CONCERN?

3.

HOW DO YOU THINK NURTURING YOURSELF WILL
BENEFIT YOUR FAMILY AND COMMUNITY?

Consequences of Neglecting Yourself

"We take better care of our smartphones
than ourselves. We know when the battery is
depleted and recharge it. We need to do the
same for ourselves."

~Arianna Huffington

*I*f increasing your awareness about the benefits of self-nurturing did not encourage you to continue reading, then let's explore the consequences of not nurturing ourselves. To begin, I wonder if you are aware when your battery needs recharging? So many people live chronically depleted and may not recognize just how great a toll it is taking. Pause for a moment and check-in with yourself. Are you currently feeling depleted, overwhelmed, or exhausted? What about stressed, frustrated, or resentful?

If you said, "yes," to any of these common consequences of neglecting yourself, it's time to recharge your battery. Running on empty leads to burnout and impacts every area of our lives. When we live in a chronic state of stress and overwhelm, we feel depleted and exhausted and may become sick, depressed, or anxious. New clients regularly share that, in addition to feeling some or all of these ways, they also suffer from headaches and physical pain. More often than not, they also feel undervalued and unappreciated by those to whom they give so much. Other consequences of neglecting ourselves include fatigue, feeling unfulfilled, indecisive, emotionally shut down, and stuck (think life on a hamster wheel). When we approach burn out, our giving cannot be sustained. That is the irony of many women's lives–giving more than they have to give and paying the price when they can no longer do so. Therefore it is crucial to notice when we feel we have given too much, and to acknowledge our symptoms as red flags. Taking this first step allows us to make more nurturing choices.

It takes courage to prioritize yourself and to choose to transform the old limiting paradigm that demands that you care for everyone in your life except yourself. That belief has led many of us to burn out, leaving us with little left to give to others and feeding our sense of not being good enough. You can learn to recognize your red flags, those symptoms that remind you that you are overextended and need to rejuvenate. Then you can make choices to increase your self-nurturing activities and refill your cup.

Common *Consequences* of Self-Neglect:

- Illness
- Exhaustion/fatigue
- Overwhelm
- Depression
- Anxiety
- Headaches
- Physical pain
- Resentment
- Feeling unfulfilled
- Lacking meaning or purpose
- Indecision
- Emotionally shut down
- Self-criticism
- Self-doubt
- Impatience
- Irritability
- Anger
- Judgmental of self and others
- Feeling stuck/hopeless
- Grief

As Eleanor Brown reminds us, "When you take time to replenish your spirit, it allows you to serve others from the overflow. You cannot serve from an empty vessel."

Reflective
Questions

1.
WHAT CONSEQUENCES OF OVEREXTENDING YOURSELF HAVE YOU EXPERIENCED?

2.
WHAT ARE YOUR RED FLAGS THAT INDICATE YOU NEED TO RECHARGE YOUR BATTERY?

3.
WHAT SYMPTOM OF SELF-NEGLECT HAVE YOU EXPERIENCED THAT WAS NOT ON THE LIST?

PART TWO

Cultivating a Self-Nurturing Practice

Cultivating Self-Compassion

"A moment of self-compassion can change your entire day. A string of such moments can change the course of your life."

~ Christopher Germer

Self-compassion is at the heart of self-nurturing and is the first step in cultivating a self-nurturing practice. To develop a loving relationship with yourself, you must begin treating yourself like you would a dear friend. Nurturing a dear friend includes being present, kind, and loving. Bringing this nurturing energy to yourself and intentionally responding with kindness and gentleness is one way to cultivate self-compassion.

As you transform your habit of self-neglect into a practice of self-nurturing, compassion will be your guide. It will inspire you to give yourself grace in the growth process rather than

41

judging yourself and expecting perfection. Self-compassion will allow you to acknowledge what you have done well, rather than looking for evidence that you are not good enough or focusing only on what you have not done. Compassion is the foundation of any sustainable change because we cannot change an un-nurturing habit from a place of blame or shame. We also cannot maintain a new habit with criticism and judgment. One empowering step you can take today is to respond to yourself with compassion and begin feeling more peace and loving kindness.

According to Dr. Kristin Neff, self-compassion researcher and expert, "Self-compassion entails being warm and understanding toward ourselves when we suffer, fail, or feel inadequate, rather than ignoring our pain or flagellating ourselves with self-criticism." I love this idea of being warm and understanding to ourselves when we suffer, fail, or feel inadequate. Choosing to respond with tenderness and kindness to yourself can decrease your suffering immeasurably. Just think about how harsh we are to ourselves when we make a mistake. That self-punishment is often worse than the original error.

If you want to assess your self-compassion, pause for a moment, and reflect on a time in the last week you made a mistake. How did you speak to yourself? Were you kind and compassionate, or did you judge and berate yourself? How did your response impact how you felt about yourself and what you did next?

If you found it was challenging to respond to yourself with compassion, you are not alone. I have witnessed that we often add to our suffering when we make mistakes or don't live up to our unrealistic expectations. We compound our shame with self-criticism and self-judgment, which decreases our ability to respond with resilience and empowerment. We get stuck in the blame and shame of ourselves and others, and, rather than learning from the mistake and growing, the experience has the potential to reinforce the notion that we are the mistake. Self-compassion reminds us that we made a mistake, but we are not a mistake.

When we are kind and compassionate toward ourselves, we take responsibility for our actions, make new empowered choices, and learn and grow from the experience. Responding in this nurturing way, helps us break the cycle of repeating the same mistakes, which further feeds our sense of unworthiness and inadequacy.

Self-compassion acts like a healing salve for our broken hearts that come from all the pain and suffering that results from being human on this planet. It allows us to use self-awareness to heal our pain rather than to reinforce that we are not good enough. It supports us in understanding that we are not alone but rather are connected to all of humanity.

When we use self-compassion, we develop self-awareness because we choose to see ourselves through the eyes of love. Self-compassion increases our trust in ourselves and positively impacts us psychologically, according to Dr. Neff's research, helping us cope effectively with life stresses and feel more hopeful. I believe self-compassion nurtures the seeds of self-awareness, self-acceptance, and self-forgiveness—all essential in transforming your habit of self-neglect.

I found self-compassion to be the self-nurturing practice that most transformed my life. I used to hold myself to such high standards and berate myself for the mistakes I made. I shamed myself each time I did not live up my unrealistic standards and gave away my peace of mind by unceasingly running through what I should have done. This habit became particularly challenging as I sought a solution to my daughter's health challenges and led to chronic anxiety, depression, and despair.

Through a self-compassion practice, I learned how to be tender towards all aspects of myself. Now, I show kindness to myself consistently and can access so much more empathy and love for myself and the world. As Pema Chödrön encourages us, "Be kinder to yourself. And then let your kindness flood the world."

Here's an exercise for you to experience what self-compassion feels like. Place your right hand on your heart. Acknowledge all the aspects of yourself that you hold dear–your kindness, generosity, playfulness, love, intelligence, curiosity, etc. Now, breathe into those parts of you with love and gratitude.

Next, place your left hand on your heart and acknowledge your challenging aspects–your judgments, criticism, anger, resentments, fear, etc. Breathe into those parts of yourself with love and compassion. For the last part of this exercise place both hands on your heart and acknowledge that all of these aspects reside within you, and each has something to teach you. Instead of rejecting any part of yourself, choose to love, and accept yourself. Through this process, you can heal your sense of unworthiness and embrace the beautiful and complex being that you are, permitting yourself to express your authenticity and truth. As Dr. Neff reminds us, "When we give ourselves compassion, we are opening our hearts in a way that can transform our lives."

44

Each time you respond to yourself with self-compassion, you nurture yourself. Begin your daily self-nurturing practice by intentionally cultivating self-compassion as it will provide the most fertile foundation for you to grow your self-awareness with love and kindness. Each act of self-compassion becomes an act of self-nurturing and reveals infinite possibilities for healing, forgiveness, and growth. Treating yourself like a dear friend reinforces your worthiness and inspires you to set boundaries so that others treat you with that same respect and love. As Jon Kabat-Zinn reminds us, "Befriending your mind, body, and heart enables you to enact a love affair with the possible." What might be possible in your life if you treated yourself like a dear friend?

Reflective
Questions

1.

WHAT OPPORTUNITIES DID YOU HAVE TO
PRACTICE SELF-COMPASSION RECENTLY?

2.

HOW DID YOU RESPOND TO YOURSELF WHEN YOU
MADE A MISTAKE?

3.

WHEN IN YOUR DAY DO YOU ESPECIALLY NEED
SELF-COMPASSION?

4.

WHAT POSITIVE IMPACT DID YOU NOTICE WHEN
YOU TREATED YOURSELF WITH MORE KINDNESS
AND COMPASSION?

Self-Nurturing

Practice Ideas

- SET AN INTENTION TO RESPOND TO YOURSELF WITH COMPASSION.

- IDENTIFY A SYMBOL THAT REMINDS YOU OF YOUR COMMITMENT TO CULTIVATE SELF-COMPASSION (LIKE A HEART, CIRCLE, INFINITY) AND DRAW IT SOMEWHERE YOU WILL SEE IT REGULARLY.

- NOTICE THROUGHOUT THE WEEK IN A SPIRIT OF CURIOSITY AND NON-JUDGMENT WHEN YOU RESPOND TO YOURSELF WITH COMPASSION AND WHEN YOU DO NOT.

- BRING AWARENESS TO YOUR SELF-TALK WHEN YOU MAKE A MISTAKE AND CHOOSE TO SPEAK TO YOURSELF LIKE YOU WOULD A DEAR FRIEND.

- WRITE AN ENCOURAGING AND LOVING LETTER TO YOURSELF AND SEND IT IN THE MAIL.

Touchstones

- WRITE YOURSELF A LOVE NOTE AND PLACE IT WHERE YOU WILL SEE IT EACH DAY.

- CREATE YOUR OWN PERMISSION SLIP TO BE COMPASSIONATE TO YOURSELF.

Affirmations

· I BREATHE AND BEGIN ANEW.

· I HAVE MADE A MISTAKE, BUT I AM NOT
A MISTAKE.

· I TREAT MYSELF WITH LOVING-KINDNESS.

Developing More Self-Awareness

"Awareness is like the sun. When it shines on things, they are transformed."

~Thich Nhat Hanh

Awareness is at the heart of transformation, as we must first become aware in order to make new choices. Although most of us know that it is impossible to give from an empty cup, many of us continue to operate from this deficit model. Since we have learned from our families and the broader culture a habit of self-neglect, we are often not aware that we are trying to pour from an empty cup. Our belief that it is our responsibility to take care of others and ensure their happiness reinforces our over-giving. When we inevitably fail, we think there is something wrong with us.

These unrealistic expectations often result in profound dis-appointment in ourselves and feed our self-criticism, judgment, and striving to do more. Once we bring more aware-ness to our patterns and our choices, we must use eyes of compassion. If we are not grounded in compassion, and our consciousness is steeped in criticism and judgment, then we'll remain stuck in our cycle of self-neglect. Self-compas-sion, coupled with self-awareness, is the most effective and loving way to bring a lens of curiosity and non-judgment to ourselves and make new nurturing choices.

If you have begun to embrace self-compassion, then you are ready to embark on the next step of cultivating a self-nurturing practice—increasing your self-awareness. At this point in the journey, remind yourself that it is almost impos-sible to pay attention to ourselves when we are caring for everyone else's needs except our own. When we live that way, it is not surprising that we lose our connection with our feelings and needs. The foundation for creating an empow-ered life filled with peace, joy, and meaning is knowing what you feel and need. Identifying what you need is fundamental to cultivate healthy relationships, set boundaries, and cre-ate your intentional life.

As we begin bringing more awareness to ourselves, we may notice that even thinking about nurturing ourselves can invoke feelings of guilt or selfishness. These feelings often stop us from nurturing ourselves and reinforce our habit of self-neglect. We may think there is something wrong with us when this happens, but in reality, it is the paradigm that no longer works and needs to be transformed. The process of transformation begins with self-awareness. As Eckhart Tolle reminds us, "Awareness is the greatest agent for change." We must bring new eyes to our giving to transform our habit of self-neglect into a practice of self-nurturing.

To assess your current self-nurturing patterns, ask yourself the following questions:

1.

DO YOU FIND YOURSELF ON THE BOTTOM OF YOUR "TO-DO" LIST, NEVER QUITE FINDING THE TIME TO TAKE CARE OF YOU?

2.

HOW OFTEN DO YOU PRIORITIZE OTHERS' NEEDS OVER YOUR OWN, LEAVING YOU FEELING CHRONICALLY OVERWHELMED AND EXHAUSTED?

3.

HOW AWARE ARE YOU OF WHEN YOU HAVE GIVEN TOO MUCH?

4.

WHAT ARE THE SIGNS THAT YOU NEED TO NURTURE YOURSELF?

5.

HOW ARE YOU FEELING RIGHT NOW, AND WHAT DO YOU NEED AT THIS MOMENT?

Most women are brilliant at recognizing other people's needs but are challenged when it comes to identifying their own. We spend so much of our time caring for other people that we lose touch with our own needs. Unfortunately, without being able to identify what we need, it is virtually impossible to get our needs met. And when we have an opportunity to nurture ourselves, we do not know where to start. As Rob Liano brilliantly points out, "If you don't know what you want, you'll never find it. If you don't know what you deserve, you'll always settle for less. You will wander, uncomfortably numb in your comfort zone, wondering how life has ended up here."

When we go for a while without getting our needs met, we become overwhelmed, exhausted, resentful, frustrated, and even depressed, lacking a sense of meaning in our lives. Have you felt any of those emotions? If so, you are not alone. By bringing awareness to your feelings, you can make different, more nurturing choices.

Learning to identify our own needs is critical for our health and wellbeing, as well as the health of our relationships. From this perspective, merely bringing awareness to and identifying our needs becomes an act of self-nurturing.

Here are four steps to determine what you need:

1.
START WITH AN INTENTION TO BE COMPASSIONATE AND NON-JUDGMENTAL TOWARD YOURSELF.

2.
CONNECT WITH YOUR BREATH AND BREATHE IN AND OUT A FEW TIMES.

3.
TUNE INTO YOUR THOUGHTS AND THE SENSATIONS IN YOUR BODY.

4.
IDENTIFY ONE NEED YOU HAVE RIGHT NOW.

Remember, no need is too small. Starting small will feed your confidence and belief in how empowering this practice can be. Just by deciding to listen to your needs, you will send a positive ripple effect throughout your life. Not only will you take better care for yourself, but you will develop your self-awareness and ability to identify your needs. That opens you up to ask for help, deeply nurture yourself, and live an empowered life filled with peace, joy, and meaning. Begin with a practice of identifying your feelings and needs at least once a day and then add to it. Once you have identified a need you have, ask yourself, "What is the most nurturing thing I could do for myself at this moment?" In the next chapter, we will move on to taking inspired action, but for now, please permit yourself to acknowledge the nurturing step you took to develop more self-awareness.

Reflective
Questions

1.

WHAT HAVE YOU LEARNED ABOUT YOURSELF BY
BRINGING MORE AWARENESS TO HOW YOU TALK
TO YOURSELF?

2.

HOW HAS CULTIVATING SELF-COMPASSION
SUPPORTED YOU IN DEVELOPING MORE SELF-
AWARENESS?

3.

WHAT MOST SURPRISED YOU WHEN YOU BROUGHT
MORE AWARENESS TO YOUR UNCONSCIOUS
HABITS?

4.

HOW DO THOSE UNCONSCIOUS HABITS FEED YOUR
HABIT OF SELF-NEGLECT?

5.

WHAT PRACTICES OF SELF-AWARENESS FELT
MOST EMPOWERING?

6.

HOW DID DEVELOPING MORE SELF-AWARENESS
EMPOWER YOU TO MAKE MORE NURTURING
CHOICES?

Self-Nurturing
Practice Ideas

- **The Arrival Technique.** Begin by bringing a spirit of curiosity and non-judgment to yourself. Close your eyes, and simply notice how it feels to be sitting in your chair. Notice your feet on the ground and where your hands are resting. Now see how it feels to breathe in deeply three times through your nose, exhaling from your mouth. Now bring awareness to your body. Notice if you feel any tension or tightness. Note if you feel any pain or discomfort. Notice if there is anywhere you feel no sensation at all. Now release the awareness of your body. Return to your breath and take three deep breaths, in and off. Now with curiosity and non-judgment, bring awareness to your thoughts. See if you can be a curious observer and label the thoughts you are having–anxious, planning, judging, etc. Now release the awareness of your thoughts and return to your breath. Remind yourself that you can connect to yourself and the present moment with your breath at any time, as it is your constant companion and best friend. Place your hand on your heart and acknowledge something about yourself that you are grateful for. On your last few intentional breaths in and out, on the in-breath say, "I breathe into this moment," and on the out-breath say, "I have arrived."

- **Mindfulness.** Practice the Arrival Technique daily to nurture your awareness of your breath, body, thoughts, and what you are grateful for about yourself to cultivate more self-awareness.
- **Eating meditation.** When you eat, bring awareness to the taste, smell, sound, texture, and gratitude for the Earth and all the people required to bring this food to you.
- **Journaling.** Try journaling at least once this week. Set a timer for 10-20 minutes and allow your thoughts to pour out onto the page. Afterward, read over your writing and notice your insights and wisdom.
- **Check-in.** Pause throughout the day to check in with yourself. How are you feeling, and what do you need? Use a timer or alert on your phone to remind you when it is time to pause and check-in.

Touchstones

· WRITE A PERMISSION SLIP TO PAUSE AND
CHECK-IN WITH WHAT YOU FEEL AND NEED AND
READ IT DAILY.

Affirmations

- I AM EMPOWERED THROUGH MY SELF-AWARENESS.

- I AM AWARE OF ALL I NEED TO MAKE NURTURING CHOICES FOR MYSELF.

- I AM OPEN AND AWARE.

- MY SELF-AWARENESS IS A POWERFUL TOOL.

- I AM GROUNDED IN SELF-AWARENESS AND SELF-COMPASSION.

Taking Inspired Action To Nurture Yourself

"Surviving is important. Thriving is elegant."

~Maya Angelou

The more you commit to cultivating a self-nurturing practice, the more you move out of survival mode and into thriving. The more you nurture yourself, the more space will be created in your life for peace, joy, and meaning. You are already well on your path to nurturing yourself by cultivating self-compassion and self-awareness. In this chapter, you will become more empowered as you learn to take inspired action to nurture yourself.

What I love about cultivating a self-nurturing practice is that it connects us deeply with ourselves and provides an opportunity to consistently nurture a relationship with ourselves. The more we learn to come home to ourselves, the more we realize that our intention of nurturing is as powerful as the activities we are engaged in. As a result, self-nurturing can elevate any activity if we bring that intention to it.

It is amazing how nurturing it can be to pause and check-in with ourselves. Introducing mindfulness, the practice of paying attention on purpose, interrupts our old habits of self-neglect. Without this pause, it is easy to get caught up in other people's needs and forget about our own. Choosing to pause and come home to ourselves is a powerful act of self-nurturing that supports us in taking inspired action. When we identify our feelings and needs it provides a springboard to take inspired action to nurture ourselves. Embodying a spirit of curiosity and non-judgment allows us to respond to our feelings and needs with loving-kindness and compassion. When you become aware of what you feel and need, the next step is taking inspired action. My favorite question is, "What is the most nurturing thing I could do for myself in this moment?"

Listening to our inner wisdom and taking inspired action to nurture ourselves builds our trust and self-confidence. If you are someone who has spent much of your life caring for others, you may not know what would be the most nurturing thing for you to do in this moment. I have worked with many clients who struggled to identify what would be nurturing. This chapter is designed to guide you through a framework to help you identify the next steps in taking inspired action and cultivating your self-nurturing practice.

The structure I offer you is a gardening metaphor. Since both self-nurturing and gardening require cultivation, this metaphor is a useful way to understand how to take inspired action. Let's explore this metaphor by looking at the soil, seeds, sunshine, water, and fertilizer of self-nurturing and asking what may require weeding in your life.

Soil. Soil is the foundation of your self-nurturing practice. You have been amending your soil with self-compassion and self-awareness and are ready to take inspired action and cultivate the next step on the journey of nurturing yourself. A gentle reminder that self-compassion and self-awareness are essential to self-nurturing and require continual intention and attention to support healthy soil to grow from.

Seeds. With a supportive foundation of cultivated soil, it is time to plant the seeds for the garden of your self-nurturing practice. Our seeds represent our intentions which will grow into our future inspired action. When you are clear about needing to nurture yourself and set a daily intention to do so, your self-nurturing practice will sprout. This self-awareness will then guide your inspired action. What self-nurturing seeds are you ready to plant?

Sunshine. The sunshine for your garden is the self-nurturing activity that you need to engage in every day. Those activities may be nourishing food, exercise, meditation, sleep, journaling, reading, hugging a loved one, intention setting, gratitude practice, pausing to connect to yourself, and being compassionate to yourself. These are the activities that light you up and restore your life energy. Although most require little time, except sleep, of course, they profoundly rejuvenate you. And what's more, you recognize you need to engage in them daily to feel filled up. What is your self-nurturing sunshine?

65

Water. Similar to sunshine, while "water" activities are deeply nurturing, you only engage in them a few times a week because they require more time and effort. Perhaps your water activity is yoga or dance class, a music lesson, being creative, walking with a friend, gardening, hiking in nature, cooking lovely meals, connecting with family and friends, playing a sport, or anything else that refreshes you. Your water may be the same activity a few times a week or a combination of activities. What is your self-nurturing water?

Fertilizer. Tina Turner reminds us, "You must love and care for yourself because that is when the best comes out." Fertilizer for your self-nurturing practice is an activity that fills you up and brings out the best in you! A fertilizer activity occurs less regularly as it requires more time and financial investment like a massage, travel, live music or a play, mindfulness retreat, vacation, or a class. You may include this activity in your self-nurturing practice every month, every few months, or annually. What would provide the fertilizer to your self-nurturing practice?

Weeding. And as every wise gardener knows, what we take out of the garden is as important as what we add. To have a thriving self-nurturing practice, we must thin out the seedlings and weed often. Our weeding may come in the form of saying "no" to things and activities that no longer serve us and "yes" to those that are more nurturing. We need to weed out our old habits of self-neglect, outdated beliefs, relationships that are not uplifting, commitments and responsibilities that stunt our growth, how we spend our time, negative self-talk, or anything that drains and disempowers us. Just as we would not weed an entire garden in one sitting, take your time weeding the garden of your life. As your awareness increases, you will notice what is not serving you and can choose to take inspired action. This practice will create ripple effects of health and positivity in your life, which will encourage you to continue. Reflect on what you are tolerating in your life. Then clarify what needs to be weeded out because it is not nurturing or supportive.

Setting boundaries is one example of weeding your garden. The more you nurture yourself, the more comfortable you will be setting limits around how you spend your time and with whom. As Elizabeth Grace Saunders reminds us, "We need to vigilantly and intentionally decide how to invest our time; otherwise, it will be spent for us." Time is a significant area to bring awareness to as you begin weeding. Self-nurturing is about prioritizing time for yourself in your life. What are you ready to weed out of your life?

Using the framework of gardening to cultivate your self-nurturing practice, choose one area to take inspired action: nourish your soil, plant seeds, radiate sunshine, water, fertilize, or weed. After you have one area firmly established, add another. As with all the chapters in this book, permit yourself to take inspired action on something you learned, but remember that there is no expectation of completing everything in the chapter at one time.

The healing power of the art of self-nurturing is that it offers you the opportunity to build your practice over time. This book is intended to support you in transforming your experience of overwhelm, not to add to it. May you embody this loving intention and nurture yourself throughout the journey, following Rumi's wisdom, "May the beauty of what you love, be what you do."

67

If you are still wondering what is the most nurturing thing you can do at this moment, reflect on what brings you joy and uplifts you. Joy is a wonderful guide to highlight what nurtures you, so compiling a list of what brings you joy can be an excellent place to start. Creating a "joy list" was how I began my self-nurturing journey. Remember, inspired action will bring energy and positive momentum as you cultivate your self-nurturing practice and will amplify your growth and potential.

Reflective
Questions

1.

WHAT BRINGS YOU JOY?

2.

WHAT ACTIVITIES DO YOU ENGAGE IN THAT
REJUVENATE AND NURTURE YOU DEEPLY?

3.

HOW DOES IT FEEL TO TAKE INSPIRED ACTION?

4.

HOW DOES THE METAPHOR OF GARDENING
SUPPORT YOU IN CULTIVATING YOUR SELF-
NURTURING PRACTICE?

5.

USING THE METAPHOR OF GARDENING, WHAT IS
YOUR SOIL, SEEDS, SUN, WATER, AND FERTILIZER,
AND WHAT REQUIRES WEEDING?

Self-Nurturing
Practice Ideas

· TAKE INSPIRED ACTION TO NURTURE YOURSELF.

· EACH DAY ACKNOWLEDGE SOME INSPIRED ACTION YOU HAVE TAKEN, NO MATTER HOW BIG OR SMALL.

· CREATE AN ACROSTIC POEM USING THE WORD "SELF-NURTURING" TO INSPIRE YOUR CONTINUED SELF-NURTURING PRACTICE.

· GROW A PLANT AS A DAILY REMINDER OF YOUR COMMITMENT TO NURTURE YOURSELF, REFLECTING ON WHAT YOU NEED IN EACH CATEGORY—SOIL, SEEDS, SUN, WATER, FERTILIZER, WEEDING.

Touchstones

- WRITE AN ACKNOWLEDGMENT NOTE CELEBRATING YOUR INSPIRED ACTION.

- CREATE A PERMISSION SLIP TO TAKE INSPIRED ACTION.

Affirmations

· I AM WORTHY.

· I LOVE AND VALUE MYSELF.

· I AM EMPOWERED TO TAKE INSPIRED ACTION TO
NURTURE MYSELF.

· I LOVE AND NURTURE MYSELF WITH EASE.

· I AM A MASTER GARDENER OF MY LIFE.

Acknowledging Self and Growth

"I try to be like a forest. Revitalizing and constantly growing."

~Forest Whitaker

A cknowledging ourselves and our growth is a powerful way to sustain positive change. After taking inspired action to nurture yourself, it is empowering to acknowledge yourself and how your practice has grown. When we celebrate our efforts and focus on what is going well in our lives, we encourage our continued growth. Acknowledging yourself then becomes a self-nurturing practice that fuels self-worth and self-confidence.

We can unplug from messages that we are not good enough when we pause to recognize our growth and reinforce our value and worth. By training ourselves to focus on what we have done rather than what we have not, we maintain our positive mindset. Imagine creating a daily "Done List" to celebrate accomplishments rather than beating yourself up for not completing your whole "to-do" list? We have choices about where we place our focus, and by practicing appreciation for your growth, you will become the most encouraging person you know!

Reflection is also a powerful way to nurture yourself. When you reflect on your experience and all you have learned, you can transform challenges into growth opportunities. Committing to this practice will permanently uproot your habit of self-neglect and inspire you to continue nurturing yourself.

Let's pause for a moment to reflect on how far you have come already. You are cultivating more self-compassion, developing more self-awareness, and taking inspired action to nurture yourself. By merely reading this book, you are nurturing yourself. Celebrate that you have chosen to transform your habit of self-neglect and cultivate a practice of self-nurturing!

The power of acknowledgment is noticing all of your efforts, not just the grand ones. When you see yourself prioritizing self-nurturing, celebrate your commitment to yourself. When you notice that you responded to yourself compassionately, celebrate that you were kind and loving to yourself. When you notice that you stopped a nurturing activity, celebrate that you are aware and invite yourself to begin anew. There is no end to your opportunities to acknowledge yourself and your growth.

Acknowledging ourselves is an essential part of cultivating resilience. According to Sheryl Sandberg and Adam Grant, who co-wrote *Option B: Facing Adversity, Building Resil-*

iency, Finding Joy, journaling daily at least five things that went well and why is one way to increase your confidence and resiliency. Research has shown that spending five-to-ten minutes a day writing about the goodness in your day can decrease stress and increase physical and mental health.

What I know is that life continues to offer all of us many opportunities to draw upon our strength and resilience. When we consistently nurture ourselves, we sustain our energetic reserves allowing us to respond to life with resilience. Acknowledging ourselves each day contributes to that reserve and our ability to be resilient, and as Oprah says, "Turn your wounds into wisdom."

May recognizing yourself and your growth become part of your daily self-nurturing practice with positive ripple effects flowing throughout your life.

Reflective
Questions

1.
HOW HAVE I GROWN THROUGH THIS PROCESS OF
CULTIVATING MY SELF-NURTURING PRACTICE?

2.
HOW HAS TREATING MYSELF WITH KINDNESS
AND COMPASSION CHANGED HOW I FEEL ABOUT
MYSELF?

3.
HOW HAS DEVELOPING MORE SELF-AWARENESS
EMPOWERED ME?

4.
WHAT DID I LEARN ABOUT MYSELF WHEN I TOOK
INSPIRED ACTION TO NURTURE MYSELF?

5.
WHAT BENEFITS HAVE I EXPERIENCED WHEN I
NURTURE MYSELF?

6.
HOW CAN I CELEBRATE MY GROWTH?

Self-Nurturing
Practice Ideas

- DEVELOP A PRACTICE OF ACKNOWLEDGING WHAT YOU HAVE DONE EACH DAY RATHER THAN FOCUSING ON WHAT YOU HAVE NOT COMPLETED.

- WRITE AND MAIL A LETTER TO YOURSELF, ACKNOWLEDGING AND CELEBRATING YOUR GROWTH.

- CREATE A "DONE LIST" AT THE END OF EACH DAY AND CELEBRATE YOUR CONTRIBUTIONS.

- WRITE DAILY IN YOUR ACKNOWLEDGMENT AND GROWTH JOURNAL.

- SPEND 5 MINUTES A DAY JOURNALING ABOUT WHAT WENT WELL IN YOUR DAY AND WHY.

Touchstones

- WRITE YOURSELF A PERMISSION SLIP TO ACKNOWLEDGE YOURSELF AND YOUR GROWTH.

- CHOOSE A JOURNAL TO BE YOUR ACKNOWLEDGMENT AND GROWTH JOURNAL.

- CREATE A "DONE" LIST.

Affirmations

· I AM EMPOWERED AND GRATEFUL.

· I AM LEARNING AND GROWING EVERY DAY.

· I ACKNOWLEDGE MYSELF AND MY GROWTH.

· I APPRECIATE MY COMMITMENT TO LOVING AND
NURTURING MYSELF.

Deepening Gratitude Practice

"There are only two ways to live life. One is as though there are no miracles and the other that everything is a miracle."

~Albert Einstein

Gratitude is a profoundly nurturing practice and has the power to transform stress, overwhelm, and negativity into peace, joy, and meaning! Deepening our gratitude practice allows us to integrate gratitude into every area of our lives, creating ripples of positivity and appreciation. By acknowledging what we are grateful for about ourselves and then introducing these practices to our families, workplaces, and communities, we focus on the blessings all around. In this process, we transform our mindsets of scarcity and overwhelm into ones of abundance and possibility.

Imagine how empowering it will be to acknowledge yourself as a miracle and blessing and embrace the practice of gratitude throughout your day!

Gratitude changes your brain chemistry, elevates your mood, and improves your overall health and well-being. Being grateful inspires you to feel more optimistic and transforms an ordinary day into one of awe and wonder. Gratitude highlights what is valuable to us and taps us into joy while fueling our motivation, enthusiasm, and inspiration. Gratitude also encourages us to learn from every experience and embrace an empowered and resilient mindset. I have found gratitude to be a lifeboat buoying me up during many storms and challenging experiences in my life. Focusing on what I am grateful for grounds me by allowing me to see the lessons in the challenges and feeling more peace, joy, love, and meaning as a result.

Alan Kaufman wrote, "Gratitude is a direct path to love for humanity." I totally agree and believe that gratitude can help us feel more connected with others and is a self-nurturing practice that can be engaged individually and in community. We can create rituals of appreciation that can inspire positivity and a culture of nurturing wherever we go.

Nina Lesowitz and Mary Beth Sammons wrote, "Many persons look at grateful people and say they are lucky or blessed, or just fortunate. But in truth, grateful people simply understand that gratitude is a signature strength. They make a point to train their gratitude muscle every day, just as if it were their heart, their mind, or their body on a treadmill." I love the idea of gratitude as a signature strength and believe that like self-nurturing it requires cultivation and care.

Here are some of my favorite gratitude practices, which you can use to strengthen your muscle and deepen your practice:

- **Commit to waking up and going to sleep with gratitude.** You can begin and end your day with three things you are grateful for to focus your attention on what is going well in your life.
- **Share gratitude at meals.** Many people begin their meals by saying grace or sharing appreciation for all the people it took to bring the nourishing food to the table. Integrate gratitude practice into all your meals and notice how it improves your mindful eating and appreciation of your food.
- **ABC's of gratitude.** One of my family's favorite gratitude practices is the ABC's of gratitude. We start at A and continue through Z, sharing something we are grateful for that begins with each letter. It is a beautiful way to connect and be creative while growing your appreciation for many different things in your life. I learn so much when I invite others to join me in this practice as it widens my experience of gratitude.
- **Birthday gratitude.** Birthdays are an excellent time to acknowledge all we are grateful for about a person. You can share your gratitude in a card, create a mason jar filled with reasons you are grateful for them, make a gratitude sign for party goers to add to, or go around at the celebration and have everyone share their appreciation of the birthday celebrant. Sharing what we are grateful for about people in our lives is the best gift we can give them!
- **Gratitude walks.** Nothing invokes gratitude more for me than a walk in nature. Whether I appreciate the beauty of the trees, clouds, birds, flowers, or magic of the changing seasons, nature allows me to connect mindfully and gratefully. Allow yourself to notice all the miracles around you while taking a gratitude walk and be open to the awe and wonder in

your life. Embody gratitude in each step and see how empowering and healing this practice becomes.

· **Transform your mood and negative conversations with gratitude.** Gratitude is an excellent antidote for a bad mood or negativity of any kind. When you notice that you have slipped into critical or judgmental thinking, shift into gratitude. Identify something in the experience you are grateful for and then add to it. Watch as your bad mood transforms into peace and joy. Remember: what we focus on grows. Also, if a group you are part of becomes gossipy or negative, shift it by honoring the challenge and then ask what they are grateful for. This allows people to reframe the difficulty into a lesson and transform their perspective from lack into abundance through gratitude. If you are not ready to engage others in this direct way, create a ripple of change by sharing what you are grateful for from a challenging experience. As a gentle reminder, this is different from "silver lining" someone else's experience, so be sure you focus on your gratitude rather than telling others what they "should" be grateful about.

· **Create communities of gratitude.** I feel passionate about the healing power of gratitude, so I have integrated a gratitude practice into many of the communities I belong to. This includes my faith community, boards of directors, staff meetings, support groups I run, workshops I facilitate, organizations I volunteer with, and gatherings of family and friends. Choose a community you can bring the healing power of gratitude to and notice the positive impact it has.

Remember what Marcus Aurelius wrote, "Within is the well-spring of good; and it is always ready to bubble up if you just dig." Gratitude connects you to the wellspring of good in your life, so start digging by recognizing the miracles all around you!

Reflective
Questions

1.

HOW DOES FOCUSING ON THE BLESSINGS IN YOUR
LIFE IMPACT HOW YOUR DAY UNFOLDS?

2.

WHAT ARE THE WAYS YOU CAN STRENGTHEN YOUR
GRATITUDE MUSCLE?

3.

HOW WOULD STRESSFUL SITUATIONS BE
DIFFERENT IF YOU UNDERSTOOD THAT GRATITUDE
WAS YOUR SIGNATURE STRENGTH?

4.

WHERE CAN YOU INCLUDE A GRATITUDE PRACTICE
IN YOUR LIFE?

5.

WHAT ARE YOU GRATEFUL FOR ABOUT YOURSELF
AND ABOUT YOUR LIFE IN THIS MOMENT?

Self-Nurturing
Practice Ideas

• CULTIVATE A GRATITUDE PRACTICE FOR WHEN YOU WAKE UP, AT MEALS, WHEN WITH COLLEAGUES, FAMILY, AND FRIENDS, WHEN LIFE IS CHALLENGING, OR WHEN YOU ARE GOING TO SLEEP AT NIGHT.

• WRITE A LETTER TO YOURSELF ACKNOWLEDGING ALL THE THINGS YOU ARE GRATEFUL FOR ABOUT YOURSELF AND YOUR LIFE AND PUT IT IN THE MAIL.

• WRITE A THANK YOU TO SOMEONE WHO HAS NURTURED OR INSPIRED YOU.

• USE A GRATITUDE JOURNAL DAILY TO ACKNOWLEDGE THE BLESSINGS IN YOUR LIFE.

Touchstones

- WRITE A PERMISSION SLIP TO BE GRATEFUL AND NOTICE BLESSINGS IN YOUR LIFE.

- WRITE THE WORD "GRATITUDE" ON A STONE AND KEEP ON YOUR DESK OR IN YOUR POCKET.

- KEEP A GRATITUDE JOURNAL WITH YOU IN YOUR PURSE, DESK, OR BAG.

Affirmations

- · I AM GRATEFUL FOR MY LIFE.

- · I AM GRATEFUL TO BE ME.

- · I CELEBRATE MY GROWTH AND BLESSINGS.

PART THREE

Integrating Self-Nurturing Practices Into Your Life

"Every artist was first an amateur."

~Ralph Waldo Emerson

There are infinite ways to integrate self-nurturing practices into your life. Now that you are becoming the artist of your own life and cultivating a self-nurturing practice, you are experiencing the benefits and know how important it is to consistently nurture yourself. This last section of the book is designed to support you by providing a menu of best practices to integrate self-nurturing into every area of your life.

Having multiple options from which to choose will empower you to find out what truly nurtures you so that you can thrive and live with more peace, joy, and meaning no matter how life unfolds. By integrating more self-nurturing practices into your life, you will inspire others and become a role model for your family and community. You have an opportunity to play an integral part in the self-nurturing evolution by inviting others to join you in nurturing activities, creating a culture of nurturing with your family, friends, and colleagues.

I am so inspired by your courage to grow and your commitment to nurture the most important relationship you will ever have - the relationship with yourself. I am honored to have walked this journey of discovery and growth with you and am so grateful for your willingness and dedication to love and care for yourself throughout the adventure. I hope you have felt nurtured along the way and find the following chapters supportive, inspiring, and empowering. Cultivating a self-nurturing practice is on-going process so please do not feel pressure to integrate all the self-nurturing options at one time. Remember one inspired action sparks the next inspired action.

Each short chapter is designed like a field guide with specific ways you can integrate self-nurturing into your life. The reflective questions will give you an opportunity to deepen your understanding of yourself, self-nurturing, and your growth. You will find the twenty-two chapters in alphabetical order from Adventure to Work and can use the index in the Table of Contents to find the topic that would most support you. You can access this information today and then can return to this section over and over as life unfolds. Thank you so much for joining me on this transformational journey!

I am sending you so much peace, love and gratitude,

Adventure

"We live in a wonderful world that is full of
beauty, charm, and adventure. There is no end
to the adventures that we can have if only we
seek them with our eyes open."

~ Jawaharlal Nehru

What I love about nurturing ourselves with adventure is that it takes us out of our routines and adds excitement and fun to our lives. Adventure also opens us up to new possibilities, inspiration, and growth. It encourages us to stretch outside our comfort zones, which can be both anxiety-inducing and exciting. Adventure is critical for our growth!

97

When we first start to nurture ourselves, that act alone may feel like an adventure. After caring for everyone else in our lives for so many years, focusing on ourselves can feel strange or even risky. Trying something new without knowing what the impact will be can bring up resistance and fear. It is normal to experience some anxiety or excitement as we embark on this new path.

But risk-taking and adventure are required if we want to grow our potential and nurture ourselves. When we choose to embrace with an open heart and mind the opportunities that arise, we undermine our resistance to change, and fear cannot take hold. Incorporating a spirit of adventure in our self-nurturing practice encourages us to see the infinite possibilities to live with more love, authenticity, joy, energy, creativity, connection, truth, and beauty!

As Eleanor Roosevelt reminded us, "The purpose of life is to live it, to taste experience to the utmost, to reach out eagerly, and without fear for newer and richer experience."

Here are *nurturing practices* to invite more adventure into your life:

- Try an activity you have not tried before.
- Be bold and do something that scares you.
- Begin a conversation with a stranger and see what you learn.
- Break your routine for one day.
- Say yes to something you would usually say no to.
- Choose curiosity over judgment.
- Be spontaneous and do something unplanned.
- Explore a new area of your town or city.
- Take a leap of faith and express yourself in a new way.
- Be creative.
- Speak your truth.
- Hike on a new path.
- Stretch outside of your comfort zone.
- Learn something new.
- Try a new food.
- Look for hidden treasures on a walk.
- Ask someone for directions to their favorite spot and check it out.
- Take a new path to a familiar place.

99

Reflective
Questions

1.

WHAT IS ONE NEW ACTIVITY YOU WILL ENGAGE IN TO NURTURE YOUR ADVENTUROUS SPIRIT?

2.

HOW WILL BEING ADVENTUROUS STRETCH YOU OUT OF YOUR COMFORT ZONE AND INSPIRE YOU?

3.

HOW COULD YOU INCLUDE ADVENTURE IN YOUR SELF-NURTURING PRACTICE?

4.

HOW COULD CHOOSING ADVENTURE BE NURTURING FOR YOU?

Aging

"The longer I live, the more beautiful life becomes."

– Frank Lloyd Wright

O ur self-nurturing practices may remain the same or may change as we age, depending on our needs and our stage of life. I included this chapter in the book as a reminder that how we nurture ourselves impacts our experience of how we age. Cultivating self-compassion is a powerful antidote for the challenges that may come during different developmental stages. Learning to listen to and prioritize our needs is invaluable as we navigate changes in the process of aging.

101

Here are a few ways to integrate *self-nurturing* practices into your life as you age:

· Acknowledge change and the aging process as normal.
· Practice self-compassion as your body and needs evolve.
· Recognize what stage of life you are in and identify the challenges and opportunities of each stage.
· Deepen your gratitude practice and identify the unexpected blessings of the stage of life you are in.
· Celebrate your growth and accomplishments.
· Let go of unrealistic expectations and beliefs that do not serve you about the aging process.
· Embrace the joy of the stage of life you are in.
· When you wake each morning, celebrate that you are alive.

Reflective
Questions

1.
WHAT IS ONE NEW WAY YOU CAN EMBRACE THE LIFE STAGE YOU ARE IN?

2.
HOW CAN YOU BE MORE COMPASSIONATE TO YOURSELF ABOUT AGING?

3.
WHAT UNEXPECTED BLESSING CAN YOU ACKNOWLEDGE THAT IS DUE TO YOUR AGE?

4.
WHAT UNREALISTIC EXPECTATION DO YOU NEED TO LET GO OF TO ENJOY THE AGE YOU ARE?

The Art of *Self-Nurturing*:

As a Couple

"Pay attention. Attention is love. And love
without attention is just a word."

~Karen Maezen Miller

*Y*ou may hold a misconception that self-nurturing is a
solo act, but that could not be farther from the truth!
Finding ways to integrate self-nurturing practices into
your life as a couple or family is critical to prioritizing self-
nurturing. When couples find ways to nurture themselves
together, their capacity to give from the overflow in their
saucers increases, and there is more love and joy in their
connection.

105

To begin, bring curiosity to your relationship and identify
activities that you both love. Then ask the question how often
do you engage in those nurturing activities? If possible, com-

mit to increasing time spent on the activities that nurture you both throughout the week. Expand your list over time and challenge yourselves to find more activities that both of you find nurturing and include them in your schedule.

Here are ways to integrate self-nurturing practices as a couple:

- Identify activities that nurture both of you.
- Be creative and try new self-nurturing activities together.
- Create a self-nurturing daily ritual as a couple, like playing a game, taking a walk, drinking tea, and talking about your day.
- Encourage each other to nurture yourselves both together and individually. Then celebrate when you do!
- Cultivate your gratitude practice together and share what you are grateful for when you wake up, at meals, on walks, and when you go to sleep.
- Learn new things about each other and the world.
- Listen with your full attention to your partner and engage in reflective listening.
- See live music, a play, or other entertainment you both enjoy.
- Cook a new meal together.
- Listen to a TED Talk, podcast, or online class and then discuss it.
- Work on a creative project together.

107

Reflective
Questions

1.

WHAT ACTIVITIES DO YOU AND YOUR PARTNER
BOTH LOVE?

2.

HOW DO YOU FEEL WHEN YOU ENGAGE IN THOSE
SELF-NURTURING ACTIVITIES TOGETHER?

3.

WHAT IS ONE NEW SELF-NURTURING PRACTICE
YOU AND YOUR PARTNER CAN TRY THIS WEEK?

4.

HOW DO YOU THINK INCORPORATING MORE
SELF-NURTURING PRACTICES AS A COUPLE WILL
IMPACT YOUR RELATIONSHIP?

Asking for Help

"Asking for help does not mean that we are weak or incompetent. It usually indicates an advanced level of honesty and intelligence."

-Anne Wilson Schaef

Asking for help is a deeply self-nurturing and transformative act. I have discovered that those who care for others often find it challenging to ask for help. Even when they feel overwhelmed, and the gift of support would make a tremendous difference to them, they may still feel uncomfortable asking for it. What I find fascinating is that most of us love to give help and feel purposeful, empowered, and joyful being able to help someone else. What stops us from asking for help and allowing someone else to contribute?

109

One way to transform your habit of self-neglect into a practice of self-nurturing, is to uncover the thoughts and beliefs that contribute to your difficulty in asking for and receiving help. Then you can transform these limiting beliefs and learn to nurture yourself, requesting what you need.

Here is a *reflective exercise* to help you identify and change limiting beliefs about asking for help:

1. Without censoring your thoughts, take a few minutes to write down what thoughts arise when you think about asking for help.
2. Reflect on your list with self-compassion and ask yourself if those thoughts are accurate.
3. If you find that your thoughts are not true, notice if they are feeding limiting beliefs you hold, like "strong, independent people do not ask for help," or "I should be able to do it all myself."
4. If you find you are hold limiting beliefs that stop you from asking for and receiving help, choose to release them and create an affirmation to replace the limiting thought.

Katerina Mayer's affirmation can inspire you to begin asking for help. "I am courageous enough to know I can accomplish great things. I am humble enough to know when to ask for help."

Embracing the self-nurturing practice of asking for and receiving help will reinforce the importance of your needs. It will also expand your support system. Each time you ask for help, you strengthen a new nurturing belief that you do not have to do it all by yourself. Asking for help also offers other people an opportunity to be supportive and nurturing to you. Choosing to perceive asking for help as a self-nurturing practice will support you in being willing to ask for help and receive it. Even if the practice is at first uncomfortable, stick with it because eventually asking for help will become a blessing for all involved.

Here are ways to begin asking for help:

- Jumpstart the process by accepting help when it is offered, even if you have not asked.
- Reflect with gratitude on the help you have received in the past and how it impacted you.
- Give yourself permission to be brave and ask for help like you would advise a dear friend to.
- Recognize your interconnectedness with others and how empowering the process of giving and receiving is in the world.
- Reach outside your comfort zone and ask for help at least one time per day and then graciously accept it.
- Remind yourself that you are loved and that asking for help allows others to show you that.
- Nurture a spirit of generosity and gratitude so that you can give and receive help with ease and grace.
- Ask for help to cultivate your support system.

Reflective
Questions

1.

WHAT DID YOU DISCOVER ABOUT YOURSELF
DOING THE REFLECTIVE EXERCISE IN THIS
CHAPTER?

2.

WHAT DO YOU STRUGGLE WITH MORE
ASKING FOR HELP OR RECEIVING IT?

3.

WHO COULD YOU ASK FOR HELP TO CULTIVATE
YOUR SUPPORT SYSTEM?

4.

WHAT IDEA WILL YOU TRY IN ORDER TO BEGIN
ASKING FOR HELP?

The Art of *Self-Nurturing*

Body

"Your body is a temple, but only if you treat
it as one."

~ Astrid Alauda

It is an empowering act of self-nurturing to love, honor, and accept our bodies just as they are. We can set a new standard for beauty–celebrating authentic beauty– and support others in this empowering process. When we give up our destructive habit of comparing and criticizing our bodies and other people's bodies, we feel more empowered and connected. We can accept and celebrate all types of bodies as beautiful.

Reclaiming our beautiful bodies is an act of self-nurturing that nourishes our self-worth and self-compassion. Healing our relationships with our bodies allows us to prioritize

115

nurturing them and motivates us to make friends with our constant companion. This can be especially difficult if we struggle with health challenges, and yet this step is critical if we are to heal and move toward wholeness. Growing your nurturing practice to include your body will support you in listening to your needs and taking inspired action. The more you befriend your body the more you will transform your unkind and unrealistic expectations of how your body should look or function and inspire others to do the same.

Nayyirah Waheed's wise words remind us of the power of nurturing our bodies. "And I said to my body, softly, 'I want to be your friend.' It took a long breath and replied, 'I have been waiting all my life for this.'"

Here are *practices* to nurture your body:

- Use the Arrival Technique (page 57) daily to tune into your body and notice with curiosity and nonjudgement where you are holding tension, tightness, pain, discomfort, or find no sensation.
- Practice yoga, stretching, and moving your body.
- Pause throughout the day to connect with and listen to your body.
- Do a body scan meditation.
- Nurture your body by being kind, loving, and compassionate when going through your daily body care routine.
- Mindfully eat nutritious food.
- Drink plenty of water.
- Exercise regularly.
- Take a walk in nature and hug a tree.
- Get a massage or give yourself a massage.
- Cultivate a daily gratitude practice for your body.
- Celebrate how your body supports you each day.
- Write down your commitment to nurturing your body.
- Acknowledge daily something you love about your body.

117

Body

- Write love notes to your body and place them around your home.
- Listen to your body and when you are tired, rest.
- Take a bath.
- Use essential oils to support and uplift you.
- Take supplements to support your body.

Reflective
Questions

1.

WHAT CONSEQUENCE HAVE YOU EXPERIENCED NOT LISTENING TO YOUR BODY?

2.

WHEN YOU LISTEN TO YOUR BODY, WHAT WISDOM DO YOU HEAR?

3.

HOW CAN YOU BRING MORE LOVE TO YOUR BODY RIGHT NOW?

4.

WHAT HAS YOUR BODY TAUGHT YOU?

5.

WHAT ARE YOU GRATEFUL FOR ABOUT YOUR BODY?

Boundaries

"Daring to set boundaries is about having the
courage to love ourselves, even when we risk
disappointing others."

~Brene Brown

Nurturing healthy boundaries is essential to nurturing
yourself. One of the ways we protect and care for ourselves is to set healthy boundaries, and these boundaries are essential to cultivating healthy relationships with
ourselves and others. To set boundaries, the guidelines of
how we want to be treated, we need to believe that we are
worthy. When we struggle with self-esteem or self-worth
issues, boundary setting can be challenging. When we do
not set healthy boundaries, we may have more experiences
that reinforce our lack of self-worth. It seems that whatever
we are willing to put up with is precisely what we will have in
our lives.

121

And the beautiful thing is we have a choice. Recognizing that we teach others how to treat us can inspire us to set and honor healthy boundaries consistently. These boundaries are critical to our self-nurturing practice as they reinforce the importance of listening to our feelings, acknowledging what we need, and prioritizing time for ourselves. As Gina Greenlee wrote, "Honoring your own boundaries is the clearest message to others to honor them, too."

If we do not enforce our boundaries, we teach people that we are not serious about them. Over time, our boundaries will be perceived as optional instead of essential. By not honoring our own boundaries, we start to lose respect for ourselves. And this undermines our relationship and trust in ourselves and contributes to our habit of self-neglect. Healthy boundaries reinforce our value and worth and create ripple effects of health and healing in our lives.

Here are ways to integrate *healthy boundaries* in your life:

- Make a list of how you want to be treated.
- Assess if you treat yourself the way you want others to treat you and, if not, start doing so.
- Regularly tune in to how you feel as a way of assessing if you need to set a boundary.
- When you feel uncomfortable in a situation, ask yourself what needs to be different.
- Set a boundary using an I-message. "I feel _____ when you _____; next time would you _____."
- Consistently reinforce your boundaries, so you learn to trust yourself and others learn to honor them.
- Know that if you have not set many boundaries in your life, this may be difficult at first.
- Be consistent with your boundaries and acknowledge your consistency as an act of self-nurturing.
- Remember, "no" is a complete sentence.
- Share with others that you are committed to setting and keeping healthy boundaries and be a role model for your family and friends.

Reflective
Questions

1.
HOW OFTEN DO YOU HONOR YOUR BOUNDARIES?

2.
WHAT IS ONE HEALTHY BOUNDARY YOU CAN
COMMIT TO THAT WILL SUPPORT YOU IN BUILDING
MORE TRUST WITH YOURSELF?

3.
WHAT WILL IT TAKE TO HONOR YOUR BOUNDARIES
CONSISTENTLY?

4.
HOW WILL NURTURING HEALTHY BOUNDARIES
IMPROVE YOUR RELATIONSHIP WITH YOURSELF
AND OTHERS?

Building Circles
of Support

"Alone, we can do so little; together, we can
do so much."

~Helen Keller

ince learning to nurture ourselves runs counter to what
our culture encourages, developing circles of support is
essential to sustaining your self-nurturing practice. These
circles will inspire you and help hold you accountable to your
self-nurturing commitments. Intentionally connecting with
others on the journey will provide essential support, enable
you to overcome obstacles, and offer you wonderful new
ideas to try. Having circles of support increase the likeli-
hood that you will continue to cultivate your self-nurturing
practice.

125

Building Circles of Support

When we share our goals with others, we are more likely to achieve them. Share your self-nurturing commitments with trusted people and invite them to check in on your progress. This added support provides structure to be consistent and accountable. Developing this kind of relationship with friends also encourages them to nurture themselves, thus spreading the empowering message of self-nurturing in the world!

Here are ways to integrate *self-
nurturing* practices into your life by
building circles of support:

- Host a book club with *The Art of Self-Nurturing.*
- Create a self-nurturing practice circle using the book as your guide.
- Invite a friend along on your self-nurturing journey.
- Ask a friend to be your accountability partner.
- Include your partner/family/friends in self-nurturing activities.
- Introduce self-nurturing practices to your colleagues at work/where you volunteer/on-line communities.
- Join an online group to give and get support around self-nurturing.

Reflective
Questions

1.
**WHO COULD BE A PART OF YOUR CIRCLE
OF SUPPORT?**

2.
WHO COULD BE AN ACCOUNTABILITY PARTNER?

3.
**WHAT GROUP ARE YOU A PART OF THAT
YOU COULD INTRODUCE SELF-NURTURING
PRACTICES TO?**

4.
**WHAT ONLINE COMMUNITY COULD YOU ENGAGE
WITH AROUND SELF-NURTURING?**

5.
**WHAT SUPPORT WOULD YOU NEED TO CREATE A
SELF-NURTURING PRACTICE CIRCLE USING THIS
BOOK AS A GUIDE?**

Caregiving

"There are only four kinds of people in the
world. Those who have been caregivers. Those
who are currently caregivers. Those who
will be caregivers, and those who will need a
caregiver."

~ Rosalyn Carter

Like many of you, I have spent my life cultivating my care-giving skills. My lessons around self-nurturing grew out of my experience of non-stop caregiving, which left me overwhelmed, exhausted, and depressed. I have so much respect for all the caregivers in the world and am dedicated to supporting them in transforming their habits of self-neglect into practices of self-nurturing. There is no more critical time to increase your self-nurturing practices than when you are taking care of others. If you want your giving to be sustainable, then you need to refill often so that you are giving from love rather than resentment.

129

Here are *self-nurturing* practices that can support you as a caregiver:

- Cultivate awareness of your own needs by journaling, talking to a trusted friend, or engaging in mindfulness practices.
- Listen to your body about what you need.
- Take breaks to meet your needs throughout the day.
- Prioritize eating meals, resting, exercising, and nurturing yourself.
- Pack a "nurturing bag" with a snack, book, extra clothes, etc. to support you while caring for others.
- Set an intention for your caregiving (like love, nurturing, kindness) to provide more meaning to the simple tasks.
- Acknowledge yourself as a caregiver and the impact you are having in the world.
- Learn to ask for help. Build a support team around you and model what it looks like to ask for help and share responsibilities. You will be more sustainable in your giving and provide others an opportunity to support you.
- Cultivate your mindfulness practice and pause throughout the day to breathe deeply and connect to the present moment.
- Nurture a non-anxious presence.

- Embrace self-compassion on your journey of helping others and be kind and loving to yourself.
- Let go of unrealistic expectations of yourself that may motivate your over-giving.
- Use the Emotional Freedom Technique or Tapping to decrease the intensity of emotions so you can remain grounded.
- Remind yourself of the importance of self-nurturing so that your giving is grounded in love rather than resentment.

Reflective
Questions

1.
WHAT MOTIVATES YOU TO CARE FOR OTHERS?

2.
HOW DO YOU KNOW THAT YOU HAVE GIVEN MORE THAN YOU HAVE TO GIVE?

3.
WHAT REJUVENATES YOU WHEN YOU HAVE GIVEN MORE THAN YOU HAVE TO GIVE?

4.
WHAT NEW SELF-NURTURING PRACTICE DO YOU COMMIT TO?

5.
WHAT MEANING DO YOU ATTRIBUTE TO YOUR CAREGIVING?

Creativity

"Your life is already artful—waiting, just
waiting for you to make it art."

~Toni Morison

*B*eing creative is deeply self-nurturing! We express our creativity when we parent, problem solve, cook, communicate, strategize, imagine, innovate, dream, and create anything in our lives. Our creativity is a well of possibility which fuels our enthusiasm, energy, joy, hope, resilience, and the feeling that anything is possible. Creativity is an empowering and nurturing way to learn about yourself, process emotions, and express yourself. Creativity provides a beautiful access point into your subconscious and opens you to new aspects of yourself, especially when you give yourself permission to turn down your inner critic. And best of all, you can be creative by yourself, with your partner, and

133

with family and friends, which makes it a fantastic self-nurturing activity!

Although creativity is a fabulous way to nurture ourselves, many people believe that they are not creative. I believe we all have an infinite amount of creativity within us, although it may not be currently cultivated or fully expressed. We may limit ourselves due to judgment of our abilities, our habit of comparing ourselves to others, and old messages we still believe about not being able to draw, paint, write, etc. As Henri Matisse so astutely reminded us, "creativity takes courage." I think it also requires a commitment to leave our inner critic at the door. So, commit today to give yourself permission to be creative and share your gifts so that your creativity can positively impact the world!

Here are ways you can integrate *self-nurturing* practices into your life through creativity:

- Draw, color, collage, paint.
- Art of any kind.
- Write or journal.
- Create a vision board or a manifestation journal.
- Sew, knit, crochet.
- Write a haiku (five syllables/seven syllables/five syllables) or other poetry.
- Play music or sing.
- Garden.
- Dance.
- Photograph.
- Build.
- Take an improv class.
- Make a card and sent it.
- Cook or bake.
- Design anything—interior/garden/yard/fashion/website.
- Share your creative ideas with others.

Reflective
Questions

1.

WHAT FORMS OF CREATIVITY DO YOU FIND NURTURING?

2.

HOW COULD YOU INCLUDE MORE CREATIVITY IN YOUR DAY?

3.

WHAT DIFFERENCE WOULD IT MAKE TO NURTURE YOUR CREATIVITY REGULARLY?

4.

WHAT CREATIVE ACTIVITIES CAN YOU INVITE OTHERS TO JOIN YOU IN?

Cultivating Resilience

"Resilience is knowing that you are the only
one that has the power and the responsibility
to pick yourself up."

~Mary Holloway

*I*n a time of continued change and uncertainty in our
world, learning to cultivate resilience is essential for
staying grounded and empowered. Resilience is our ability
to bounce back from difficult experiences, and like self-nurturing can be intentionally cultivated over time to create a
reserve to draw upon.

I am grateful for Sheryl Sandberg and Adam Grant's book,   137
Option B: Facing Adversity, Building Resilience, and Finding
Joy, and their definition that "Resilience is the strength and
speed of our response to adversity and we can build it. It

isn't about having a backbone. It is about strengthening the muscles around our backbone."

I love the idea of strengthening the muscles around our backbone since this is a more empowering approach than judging ourselves as either weak or strong and reminds us that cultivating resilience is a practice. Recognizing that we can nurture resilience within ourselves and intentionally improve our ability to bounce back from disappointments, losses, and failure is empowering and nurturing.

Martin Seligman, a pioneer of positive psychology and author, wrote that "We plant the seeds of resilience in the ways we process negative events." He defined three ways we often undermine our ability to overcome difficult situations, which he calls the 3 P's: personalization, pervasiveness, and permanence. When we view a problem as our fault, see it everywhere in our lives, and believe that it will always be that way, we stay stuck in the problem. I find the 3 P's a wonderful framework to understand what is stopping us from being resilient, as well as a guide to transform these limiting perceptions.

Here are *self-nurturing* practices to cultivate your resilience:

- Notice with gratitude what is good in your life.
- Develop your capacity to acknowledge and affirm the pain you are feeling.
- Allow yourself time and space to grieve.
- Embrace self-compassion–remember you may have made a mistake, but you are not a mistake.
- Be mindful of what you say to yourself– limit words like "always" and "never" that reinforce permanence and change to "sometimes" or "lately" to support yourself in seeing more possibilities and the potential for healing or transformation.
- Journal daily.
- Acknowledge what is going well in your life and why for five-to-ten minutes each day.
- Ask for help.
- Nurture yourself every day.
- Remind yourself of Maya Angelou's wise words, "I can be changed by what happens to me. But I refuse to be reduced by it."

139

Reflective
Questions

1.
**WHAT HAVE YOU LEARNED FROM THE
CHALLENGES YOU HAVE OVERCOME?**

2.
**WHAT SKILLS AND TOOLS DID YOU USE TO
OVERCOME THEM?**

3.
**HOW HAVE YOU GROWN AS A RESULT OF THESE
CHALLENGES?**

4.
**WHAT IS GOING WELL IN YOUR LIFE RIGHT NOW,
AND WHY?**

5.
**HOW DO YOU SPEAK TO YOURSELF ABOUT
CHALLENGING SITUATIONS?**

6.
WHEN IS THE LAST TIME YOU ASKED FOR HELP?

7.
**WHAT CAN YOU ACKNOWLEDGE ABOUT YOURSELF
IN THIS MOMENT?**

Family

"Mindful parenting is the hardest job
on the planet, but it's also one that has
the potential for the deepest kinds of
satisfactions over the life span, and the
greatest feelings of interconnectedness and
community and belonging."

~Jon Kabat Zinn

*P*arenting has been one of the best and hardest jobs of my life. My daughters are my best teachers, and I am so grateful for everything I have learned about self-nurturing as a result of parenting them. As I reminded you in the chapter on integrating self-nurturing as a couple, self-nurturing does not need to be a solo act. You can adapt any of the practices in this book to incorporate self-nurturing practices as a family. Practicing together can strengthen a family and model these essential lessons for children early in their lives. When children understand the importance of nurturing themselves by engaging in self-nurturing activi-

141

ties together as a family, they will know their self-worth and value and understand the meaning of giving from the over-flow in their saucer rather than the last drops in their cup. As Michelle Obama reminds us, "With every word we utter, with every action we take, we know our kids are watching us. We, as parents, are their most important role models."

Here are ways to engage in *self-nurturing* practices with your family:

- Have fun together.
- Play games together.
- Take walks together.
- Eat meals together.
- Clean up together.
- Share gratitude and love.
- Meditate together.
- Be creative together.
- Make music together.
- Develop a gratitude wall in your house.
- Create a family self-nurturing list.
- Schedule nurturing activities together as a family.
- Dance or exercise together.
- Give each other permission and the time and space to nurture yourselves individually and as a family.
- Celebrate self-nurturing in your family.
- Find creative ways to include family virtually by phone or computer.
- Write letters and stay connected to family members.
- Create a family self-nurturing challenge.

143

Reflective
Questions

1.

WHAT ACTIVITIES DOES YOUR FAMILY ENJOY
DOING TOGETHER?

2.

WHAT NURTURING PRACTICE CAN YOU ENGAGE IN
AS A FAMILY EVERY DAY?

3.

WHAT DO YOU LOVE AND APPRECIATE ABOUT
YOUR FAMILY?

4.

HOW CAN YOU SUPPORT EACH OTHER IN
NURTURING YOURSELVES INDIVIDUALLY AND
AS A FAMILY?

Fun

"There's no fear when you're having fun."

~Will Thomas

H ave you experienced the incredible power of laugh-
ter and fun to bring you effortlessly into the present
moment? What I love about having fun is that our attention is
focused on the present moment, and our concerns and anxi-
eties seem to melt away. When we are mindful and having
fun, we are not stuck in regret about the past or fear about
the future, and our experience of joy, peace, and happiness
increase. Nurturing ourselves by having fun is a wonderful way to integrate self-nurturing practices into our lives.
Although it may feel challenging to invite more fun into your
day when you are feeling overwhelmed and exhausted, you
will quickly find that fun is exactly the antidote you need.

To begin, invite a spirit of curiosity, wonder, and joy into your day. Then identify what is fun for you and permit yourself to include it in your day. If you are struggling to make it happen, schedule fun in your calendar, so you prioritize time for fun. You will enjoy the stress-relieving benefits of fun right away, and over time, you will find more opportunities to have more fun each day. The great thing about fun is that it can be spontaneous and take only moments or be planned and take the whole day. The choice is yours!

Here are ways to integrate
the *nurturing* practice of fun into
your life:

- Give yourself permission to be spontaneous and playful.
- Play board games with family or friends.
- Walk in nature or on the beach and notice all the beauty around you.
- Play with children or pets.
- Dance to music you love.
- Laugh with a friend.
- Play a sport.
- Smile at people throughout your day.
- Ride a bike.
- Write a gratitude list.
- Create a "fun" list and engage in activities daily.
- Acknowledge what fun activities you enjoyed in the past week.
- Create a "fun activity jar" with ideas you can pull from for a spontaneous experience of fun.

Reflective
Questions

1.

HOW OFTEN DO YOU ALLOW YOURSELF TO HAVE FUN?

2.

WHAT DID YOU ENJOY DOING AS A CHILD THAT YOU STILL FIND FUN TODAY?

3.

WHAT IS YOUR FAVORITE WAY TO BE SPONTANEOUS?

4.

HOW CAN YOU HAVE MORE FUN WITH YOUR PARTNER, FAMILY, AND FRIENDS?

5.

WHAT NEW WAY(S) WILL YOU INVITE MORE FUN INTO YOUR LIFE?

6.

HOW WILL HAVING FUN NURTURE YOU?

Healing from Illness and Injury

"Nurturing yourself is not selfish—it's essential to your survival and your well-being."

~Renee Peterson Trudeau

Having supported my daughter for years through chronic health challenges, I know how overwhelming illness and injuries can be. There is often a feeling of being out of control while trying to navigate the many unknowns. It is stressful enough to be sick or injured but add all the other stressors of missed work/school, doctor appointments, insurance, pain, exhaustion, and complete life disruption, and it is not surprising that we can become stressed out and overwhelmed. And this experience of overwhelm is not only experienced by the person who is sick, but also by those who love, care for, and support them. Fortunately, self-nur-

149

turing practices can transform the experience of being ill or injured and can help us improve our quality of life in the recovery process.

Here are some ways to integrate *self-nurturing* practices when you are healing:

- **Prioritize Your Healing.** Often when we are responsible for caring for everyone else in our lives, we do not prioritize our own healing. Choosing to prioritize your healing is the foundation of nurturing yourself through illness and injury and provides space in your life to attend to your needs.
- **Be Kind to Yourself.** Instead of being critical and judgmental of yourself, choose to treat yourself like you would a dear friend and love and nurture yourself through the healing process.
- **Give yourself permission to do the most nurturing thing you can do at this moment.**
- **Rest.** "We humans have lost the wisdom of genuinely resting and relaxing. We worry too much. We don't allow our bodies to heal, and we do not allow our minds and hearts to heal." Thich Nhat Hanh.

Often, our illness and injury last longer when we do not rest. Rest is a magic elixir that offers profound healing in almost every situation. Give yourself permission to rest while you are recovering from illness or injury or are caring for someone who is.

151

- **Eat Nourishing Food and Drink Plenty of Water.** This can be tricky if you are hospitalized or unable to cook for yourself. Bring mindfulness to what you put into your body and choose foods that support your immune system, mood, energy level, and fuel your recovery.
- **Ask for Help.** There is no better time to start building your receiving muscles then when you are sick or injured. Nurture your support system by asking for help, and you will bless yourself and the giver with this act of self-nurturing.
- **Meditate/Pray.** Cultivating the self-nurturing practice of meditation and prayer can be deeply supportive to your healing process. Meditation intentionally connects you to your breath and body and supports you in decreasing stress, pain, and overwhelm. Prayer connects you to a source greater than yourself and supports you in feeling loved, protected, and genuinely cared for.
- **Acknowledge What is Going Well and Strengthen Your Gratitude Practice.** One way we can cultivate resilience, which is so needed in the healing process, is to acknowledge what is going well and what we are grateful for in our lives. Choosing to focus on what is going well will prime your brain for the positive and uplift your mood. Recognizing what you are grateful for will change your brain chemistry and neural pathways and is nurturing and healing.

Reflective
Questions

1.

WHAT STOPS YOU FROM PRIORITIZING YOUR
HEALING WHEN YOU ARE SICK OR INJURED?

2.

HOW HAVE YOU NURTURED YOURSELF PREVIOUSLY
WHEN YOU WERE SICK OR INJURED?

3.

WHAT NEW SELF-NURTURING PRACTICES WILL
YOU ENGAGE IN TO SUPPORT YOUR HEALING?

4.

WHO COULD YOU REACH OUT TO AND ASK
FOR HELP?

5.

WHAT IS GOING WELL IN THIS MOMENT AND WHAT
ARE YOU GRATEFUL FOR?

The Art of *Self-Nurturing*

Health and Well-being

> "Caring for your body, mind, and spirit is your greatest and grandest responsibility. It's about listening to the needs of your soul and then honoring them."
>
> ~Kristi Ling

Nurturing our health and well-being are foundational to cultivating a self-nurturing practice. Bringing love, tender care, and compassion to our bodies is an essential way to nurture our vibrant health and well-being. If you are looking for ways to integrate more self-nurturing practices into your life to foster health and well-being, you are in luck because most nurturing activities will improve your health and well-being.

155

Here are ways to integrate *self-nurturing* practices into your life to cultivate health and well-being:

- **Listen to your body.** Paying attention to your body allows you to make healthy choices and nurture yourself before you get sick.
- **Meditate.** Research shows that meditation has incredible benefits for the mind, body, and spirit. As a bonus, when you meditate regularly, you become more self-aware and make healthier choices for yourself.
- **Get out in nature.** Most people experience a deep sense of peace being in nature and feel a sense of interconnectedness with the world. Take a few minutes to walk outdoors, notice the trees, plants, and life around you to feel refreshed and rejuvenated.
- **Cultivate a gratitude practice.** Acknowledging the blessings in your life is profoundly nourishing and changes your mood and perspective. Create a practice for sharing what you are grateful for and notice how your mind, body, and spirit respond when you approach the world with a grateful heart. Gratitude promotes vibrant health.
- **Be creative.** Like being in nature, creativity connects and nourishes your mind, body, and spirit in a joyful, easy way. Express yourself by drawing, coloring, collaging, painting,

decorating your home or office, gardening, writing, dancing, singing, or playing an instrument to nurture yourself.

· **Write a love note.** Engage in the nurturing practice of expressing love to yourself and others! Writing love notes is a fun and nurturing way to spread love and kindness in the world. Start by writing a love note to yourself, acknowledging your love and appreciation for you. Next, leave a love note for your beloved family member or friend and let them know how much they mean to you. Giving and receiving love promotes vibrant health.

· **Mindfully eat food you love.** The practice of mindful eating is not only empowering, but research shows that mindful eating supports healthy food choices, creates more awareness of portion size, and increases your appreciation of food. To start, decide to eat one meal without distractions of technology or phones and bring your total awareness and all your senses to the experience of eating.

· **Play.** Creating unstructured time to play is so essential for your vibrant health. Whether you are playing board games (my family's favorite), a sport, or playing on the floor with children or your dog, allowing yourself time to play and be in the moment is essential for living with more peace, joy, and well-being.

Reflective
Questions

1.

WHICH SELF-NURTURING PRACTICES WILL YOU INCLUDE IN YOUR DAY TO NURTURE YOUR HEALTH AND WELL-BEING?

2.

WHERE IN YOUR DAY COULD YOU SCHEDULE THESE NURTURING PRACTICES?

3.

HOW COULD YOU PRACTICE LISTENING TO YOUR BODY TO MAINTAIN YOUR HEALTH AND WELL-BEING INSTEAD OF WAITING UNTIL YOU ARE SICK?

4.

HOW CAN YOU PRIORITIZE YOUR HEALTH AND WELL-BEING?

5.

WHAT WOULD YOUR LOVE NOTE TO YOURSELF SAY?

Holidays

"Taking care of yourself doesn't mean me
first; it means me too."

~L.R. Knost

For many people, the holidays are filled with family,
friends, festivities, and fun. But for others, holidays may
feel stressful and challenging, highlighting loneliness, dis-
appointment, and loss. Whether you have waited for a holiday all year long or cannot wait for it to be over, nurturing
yourself is the key. Finding ways to stay grounded as you
navigate the holidays is a foundation of cultivating peace
and joy and transforming stress and overwhelm.

Here are ways to integrate *self-nurturing* practices into your life during the holidays:

- **Start the day out with your most self-nurturing practice.** If you know that exercise, meditation, or acknowledging what you are grateful for is your most nurturing practice, choose to begin your day that way. Prioritize ten minutes in the morning for your most nurturing practice. The more filled up you are from the start, the more energy, patience, and perspective you will have as your day unfolds.
- **Simplify your holiday experience.** There are many ways to simplify the holidays, including choosing not to over-commit. Be intentional about the invitations you accept. Invite others to help with food at holiday parties you host. Simplify your gift-giving by purchasing gift cards or donating to a meaningful cause in someone's name. Cultivate a "choose to" mindset rather than feeling pressured by a "have to" mindset and create more peace and ease in your life.
- **Create time each day for self-reflection.** Nurturing ourselves requires that we know what we need and then make supportive choices for ourselves. This is important at any time of year, but especially during

holidays. Spend some time each day cultivating your self-awareness by journaling, meditating, creating a list of things you appreciate about yourself and your life, and pause to breathe and connect with yourself in the present moment. What a difference an intentional breath can make!

· **Be sure to include play in your holiday experience.** Play is such a powerful self-nurturing strategy and allows us to connect with ourselves, others, and the present moment. Finding ways to release stress and increase joy by being playful and having fun is healing and transformative. You can play board games, watch holiday movies, dance, hula-hoop, take a walk, bake your favorite holiday dessert, and be creative all in the spirit of playfulness.

· **Set an intention for peace and joy for the holiday.** Intention setting is a powerful tool that can transform your experience. Choose to cultivate peace and joy by nurturing yourself consistently and embodying the true meaning of the holiday. When you feel nurtured, you will be able to spread more love, kindness, and compassion in the world with endless positive effects.

Reflective
Questions

1.

WHAT DO YOU FIND STRESSFUL ABOUT
HOLIDAYS?

2.

HOW COULD NURTURING YOURSELF TRANSFORM
THAT STRESS?

3.

HOW COULD YOU INCLUDE MORE FUN AND
PLAYFULNESS IN YOUR HOLIDAY PLANNING?

4.

WHAT NURTURING INTENTION FOR THE HOLIDAY
COULD YOU EMBODY?

Mindfulness

"Mindfulness is a radical act of love, sanity, kindness, and becomes our north star."

~Jon Kabat-Zinn

The definition of mindfulness is to pay attention on purpose with curiosity and non-judgment. Practicing mindfulness empowers us to nurture peace in the world from the inside out. As Thich Nhat Hanh reminds us, "Our capacity to make peace with another person and the world depends very much on our capacity to make peace with ourselves." Mindfulness deepens our self-awareness and allows us to be more accepting, compassionate, and kind to ourselves and others. When we are more connected with ourselves, we make more empowered self-nurturing choices. Over time, we create the space needed in our lives to make choices to

163

respond rather than react. The more we cultivate mindfulness, the more we model an intentional and peaceful way of living together, impacting all our relationships.

I am so grateful to Jon Kabat-Zinn and the Mindfulness-Based Stress Reduction Program he developed over thirty-five years ago at the University of Massachusetts Medical Center for highlighting the amazing benefits of mindfulness and spearheading research on the brain and mindfulness. As a result, we have compelling research to show that mindfulness decreases stress, increases self-awareness, deepens your quality of life, lowers blood pressure, and boosts your immune response. Regular mindfulness practice grows your prefrontal cortex improving your concentration, focus, memory, and emotional processing. Mindfulness is a foundation of self-nurturing and strengthens your empathy, decreases depression and anxiety, and offers a path to greater happiness and well-being in the present moment.

Here are ways to integrate
mindful *self-nurturing* practices
into your life:

- Start by pausing and connecting with your breath throughout the day, working up to ten intentional breaths at a time.
- Use the Arrival Technique shared on page 57 whenever you need to ground and center yourself.
- Bring a spirit of curiosity and non-judgment to how you are feeling and what you are thinking.
- Use the STOP mindfulness practice, which invites you to stop, take a breath, observe, and then proceed.
- Develop more body awareness by checking in with your body when you have a strong emotional reaction and identifying where you are holding that emotion.
- Choose to eat a meal mindfully and enrich your experience by noticing all you can about your food.
- Take a walk and notice the beauty around you.
- Meditate daily.
- Listen to guided meditations online or on a phone app.
- Put your phone away and be present and mindful of those with whom you are interacting.
- Notice all the blessings that already exist in your life.

Reflective
Questions

1.
WHAT BENEFITS OF MINDFULNESS MOTIVATE YOU TO INCLUDE MORE PRACTICES IN YOUR DAY?

2.
WHICH MINDFULNESS PRACTICES WILL YOU TRY?

3.
HOW COULD YOU INCLUDE BREATHING INTENTIONALLY THROUGHOUT YOUR DAY?

4.
HOW WILL BEING MORE MINDFUL IMPROVE YOUR RELATIONSHIPS?

5.
HOW COULD INTEGRATING MINDFULNESS PRACTICES INTO YOUR DAY NURTURE YOU?

Moving Through Grief

"Darkness cannot drive out darkness; only light can do that. Hate cannot drive out hate; only love can do that."

~Martin Luther King, Jr.

Although it is essential to nurture yourself regularly to keep your cup full, it is especially important to nurture yourself during difficult and challenging times. When our coping skills are overwhelmed with grief and loss like after a death of a loved one, illness, divorce, loss of a job, moving, or anything other major transition, our reserves are usually depleted. Coping with these challenges requires increased self-nurturing.

Grief has a way of knitting itself into the texture of your day and permeating your existence, like dark ink dropping onto the fabric of your day. Grief can be a very isolating experience,

167

as it leaves you feeling raw and vulnerable and unable to interact in normal activities. Grief's companion is fear, which tends
to be invasive, weaving itself into our thinking, undermining
our peace of mind, and increasing our anxious thoughts and
concerns about what is going to happen next. It is especially
crucial to self-nurture when you experience grief and fear.
And although challenging, it is essential to find gentle ways to
nurture yourself during these difficult times.

Here are ways to integrate *self-nurturing* practices when you are moving through grief:

- Start by looking at your self-nurturing practice to see if there are any activities you can continue. Having some connection to your regular schedule can be very grounding. If you take a walk each day, meditate or write in a journal, continue doing so, even for five to ten minutes daily.
- Bring mindfulness to the choices you make about what to eat. During this time, it is crucial to choose healthy food filled with nutrients and energy while minimizing food and drink that deplete you.
- Identify a few activities that feel profoundly nurturing. Perhaps you find walking in nature, talking to a supportive friend or loved one, petting your animal, reading an inspiring book, or appreciating music, art, or beauty to be nourishing. Create a "nurturing list" to make remembering these activities easier.
- Encourage yourself to engage in nurturing activities a few times during the week and notice how you feel afterward. Sometimes, it is incredibly difficult to motivate yourself to go out and do anything when you are overwhelmed with grief and loss, but most of us feel better for doing it.

169

- Ask for help and support. Feeling isolated and alone in your grief is normal, so reach out to others for comfort so you can be reminded that you are loved and cared about.
- Bring more kindness and compassion to yourself and honor your feelings.
- Find some way to feel that you are making the world a better place. Spread kindness and compassion by spending loving time with family, volunteering, or contributing in any way that makes you feel that you are having a positive impact in the world.

Reflective
Questions

1.

HOW CAN YOU NURTURE YOURSELF WHEN YOU
ARE GRIEVING?

2.

WHAT IS ONE STEP YOU CAN TAKE TO NURTURE
YOURSELF TODAY?

3.

WHO CAN YOU REACH OUT TO FOR SUPPORT?

4.

HOW WILL YOU BE KINDER AND MORE
COMPASSIONATE TO YOURSELF?

Rebuild Self-Trust by Scheduling Self-Nurturing

"Motivation is what gets you started.
Commitment is what keeps you going."

~Jim Rohn

Any time we make a change in our lives, we need tools to support the new habit to take root and become part of our new normal. I have found that at the heart of cultivating sustainable change is choice. Every time we choose to give our attention to our intentions, we further our commitment to growth in our lives. Motivation is sparked by the possibilities embodied in choice, and commitment is sustained by inspired action through our everyday choices.

When we do not prioritize time for ourselves and break our commitments to ourselves, we undermine our self-confidence and self-worth. When this happens consistently, we

173

create a powerful cycle that makes nurturing ourselves even more difficult. We may feel guilty or bad about ourselves for not following through with our commitments, which fuels our belief that we are not good enough. These feelings of unworthiness then stop us from nurturing ourselves and reinforce the idea that to have value we must first care for everyone else in our lives, leaving little time for us. It is easy to get stuck in this cycle of overwhelm and exhaustion, but it does not have to be that way. We can choose to break the cycle by reestablishing trust with ourselves and keeping our self-nurturing intentions

Here are ways to rebuild trust with yourself and integrate *self-nurturing* practices in your life by putting them in your schedule:

- Begin with self-compassion and self-forgiveness. If you have broken your commitment to yourself, recognize that you made a mistake, but you are not a mistake. Forgive yourself for not following through and start anew.
- Remember, there is no need for perfection on this journey of self-nurturing. You have an opportunity to see this experience as a lesson about the growth process and welcome your new awareness with gratitude. Bring attention to what choices you are making about how you spend your time.
- Make a commitment to yourself about how often you will nurture yourself. Define how many times you will engage in your self-nurturing practice during the day, week, or month, like meditating for five-to-ten minutes daily. Be specific, so you know what commitment you are making to yourself and can hold yourself accountable with love and kindness.
- Place your self-nurturing intention on your calendar. To reinforce your commitment and renew your trust in yourself, prioritize time in your schedule for your new practice.

175

Rebuild Self-Trust by Scheduling Self-Nurturing

Designate time on your calendar for whatever length of time you are committing. If you use an electronic calendar, include an alert to support you in fulfilling your commitment to yourself.

· Acknowledge your growth and effort. For many of us, we can easily recognize when we fall short but are challenged to acknowledge our progress and growth. Part of cultivating a self-nurturing practice is learning to acknowledge yourself, your inspired action, and your growth. You have the power to grow your acknowledgment muscle by identifying your growth and positive choices every day.

Reflective
Questions

1.

DOES YOUR CALENDAR REFLECT YOUR INTENTIONS AND COMMITMENT TO BE MORE NURTURING TO YOURSELF?

2.

DO YOU HAVE TIME PRIORITIZED FOR YOUR SELF-NURTURING ACTIVITIES?

3.

DO YOU SCHEDULE A TIME FOR THOSE ACTIVITIES IN YOUR CALENDAR?

4.

IF SOMEONE ELSE PICKED UP YOUR CALENDAR, WOULD THEY BE ABLE TO ASSESS WHAT YOU VALUE BY HOW YOU SPEND YOUR TIME?

5.

WHAT HAVE YOU LEARNED ABOUT YOURSELF AND HOW YOU HAVE GROWN?

Staying Grounded in Challenging Times

"Keep walking through the storm. Your
rainbow is waiting on the other side."

~Heather Stillufsen

When life offers us challenges to overcome, acting from faith, and not fear is a powerful choice. Choosing faith over fear requires that we cultivate belief, positive expectation, mindful presence, and trust. Since we know that fear can limit our ability to take inspired action, it is critical to ground ourselves and embrace faith in our process of growth. Cultivating faith and belief in ourselves are self-nurturing choices that empower us to grow. We may not be able to avoid crises in life, but we can develop self-nurturing practices to navigate them with ease and grace. Since there

179

are so many things outside our control, learning to trust our ability to negotiate, address, and handle challenges that may arise is how we develop confidence in ourselves and the world.

Here are ways to integrate *self-nurturing* practices to stay grounded during challenging times:

- Pause, breathe, and check-in with your body to ground yourself. Take a few deep calming breaths to center yourself and feel your feet on the ground.
- Return home to yourself by placing your hand on your heart when you feel overwhelmed by chaos outside yourself.
- Use the STOP mindfulness practice, which invites you to stop, take a breath, observe, and then proceed.
- Connect with your spirituality.
- Go for a mindful walk to ground and center yourself. Connect to the awe and wonder around you by watching the clouds, enjoying the birds and nature, and feeling your interconnection with the world.
- Walk barefoot on the earth to ground yourself or walk near the water.
- Rest, eat healthy food, exercise, and care for your body.
- Journal to process your feelings and affirm and acknowledge yourself.
- Clarify what is important to you, and then choose to make decisions with that in mind.
- Listen to music that is calming or uplifting.
- Soak in a bath.

181

Staying Grounded in Challenging Times

· Listen to what you need and make nurturing choices.
· Focus on the unexpected blessings in this time of change.

Reflective
Questions

1.
WHAT STRATEGIES WILL YOU USE TO STAY
GROUNDED IN CHALLENGING TIMES?

2.
WHAT IS ONE THING YOU CAN DO TO CULTIVATE
FAITH IN YOURSELF TODAY?

3.
HOW DOES YOUR ABILITY TO COME FROM BELIEF,
POSITIVE EXPECTATION, AND TRUST SUPPORT
YOU IN GROWING?

4.
HOW WOULD YOUR PROCESS OF GROWTH CHANGE
IF YOU INTENTIONALLY STAYED IN FAITH RATHER
THAN FEAR?

5.
WHAT UNEXPECTED BLESSING HAS COME OUT OF
THIS CHALLENGING TIME?

183

Transitions and Life Changes

"How do you know that the side you are used
to is better than the one to come?"

~Rumi

Life is filled with many transitions and life changes. To stay
grounded amid change and not resist it, we must honor
the loss we are experiencing. When we acknowledge the
loss that occurs with every significant change in our lives,
we can then open to the possibility of something better on
the other side. Honoring loss and the emotions that arise
are critical for our self-awareness, growth, and healing.

Transitions are stressful for many reasons, including that
they bring a loss of an old identity and a journey into the
unknown. Most of us feel anxious when it comes to the
unknown. We can feel overwhelmed by the pressure of all

the decisions that need to be made. Since change is a consistent companion on this journey of life, understanding the grief and loss that comes with it is critical to understanding the importance of nurturing ourselves through the process.

Although change can be deeply unsettling, we can remain grounded by acknowledging the loss, processing our emotions, and then looking to the infinite possibilities in front of us. We can choose not to resist the change but instead turn toward the possibilities that change provides in our lives.

Here are ways to integrate *self-nurturing* practices into your life during transitions:

- Allow yourself to feel the pain, loss, and disappointment of the change.
- Honor your emotions instead of rejecting or ignoring them.
- Embrace self-compassion and quiet your inner critic.
- Journal about the change, exploring and affirming your ambivalent feelings.
- Acknowledge what you have learned from this transition or change.
- Identify the hidden blessings in the change.
- Continue the self-nurturing practices that ground and connect you to yourself.
- Remember that change is part of life and that you have the tools to navigate it.
- Ask for help and support to remind yourself that you are not alone and you are loved.

Reflective
Questions

1.

WHAT LOSSES MIGHT YOU NEED TO HONOR AND
GRIEVE ABOUT THIS TRANSITION AND CHANGE?

2.

WHAT CONFLICTING EMOTIONS ARE YOU HOLDING
ABOUT THIS TRANSITION?

3.

HOW CAN YOU SHOW YOURSELF COMPASSION
AND LOVING-KINDNESS AS YOU HONOR YOUR
GRIEF AND PROCESS YOUR FEELINGS?

4.

HOW WILL YOU NURTURE YOURSELF THROUGH
THIS TRANSITION?

Traveling

"A journey of a thousand miles must begin with a single step."

~Lao Tzu

Traveling can be a deeply nurturing experience. Visiting new places, exploring, and learning about ourselves and the world can feel very nurturing, but travel can also be stressful as we stretch outside our comfort zones. Often, by the time we leave for a trip, we are stressed out and exhausted. Instead of being kind to ourselves and planning mindfully, we schedule early morning flights, close connections, and full schedules. Sometimes we travel for vacations and other times we travel for work, so there are different stresses as a result.

189

Here are ways to integrate *self-nurturing* practices when you travel:

- When planning your trip, set an intention to nurture yourself.
- Schedule your transportation so that it is a nurturing experience.
- Create a list of nurturing activities to engage in when you have time traveling.
- Give yourself permission to engage in new nurturing activities.
- Continue your morning and evening self-nurturing practices while on your trip.
- Create time to sleep, dream, rest, play games, read, journal, meditate, write a letter, talk, and/or watch a movie while traveling.
- Commit to exercise while traveling.
- Pack a "nurturing bag" with items that will support you during your travels.
- Schedule a day off when you return home, so you have time to transition back and reconnect with your family.
- Create a communication plan with your partner and family to stay connected when you are apart.

Reflective
Questions

1.

HOW CAN YOU PLAN YOUR TRAVEL SO THAT IT WILL BE A NURTURING EXPERIENCE?

2.

WHAT DO YOU NEED TO GIVE YOURSELF PERMISSION TO DO WHEN YOU ARE TRAVELING?

3.

WHAT WOULD MAKE THE MOST NURTURING IMPACT WHEN YOU TRAVEL?

4.

WHAT NEW NURTURING PRACTICES WILL YOU ENGAGE IN WHEN TRAVELING?

191

Work

"In my own deepening understanding of myself, I find my capacity to serve others is deepened as well. The better I am at self-care, the more genuinely nurturing of others, I am able to be."

~Mary Anne Radmacher

We have the power to cultivate a culture of wellness and self-nurturing in our places of employment. I feel deeply grateful to provide self-nurturing and mindfulness workshops to organizations making the world a better place because I know the impact self-nurtured people can have on the world. When organizations support their employees in nurturing themselves, they have more present, energized, productive, healthy, invested, and positive employees. The more organizations value self-nurturing, the more they will prioritize policies and practices that empower employees

193

and fuel team building, healthy communication, boundaries, and overall health and wellness. I hope you will be the spark in your organization to inspire a culture of self-nurturing where everyone benefits!

Here are ways to integrate *self-nurturing* practices in your place of work:

- Add time for gratitude practice to the meeting agendas, where you invite people to share what they are grateful for.
- Positively acknowledge those who nurture themselves.
- Prioritize breaks throughout the day, including lunch.
- Invite a massage therapist to provide massage on-site.
- Find a yoga instructor or meditation teacher to offer classes for employees.
- Post nurturing workshops and free nurturing activities happening in the community in your breakroom or on-line forums.
- Create nurturing spaces for people to take breaks both inside and outside, if possible.
- Start a gratitude wall in your office for people to write down what they are grateful for and build a culture of gratitude.
- Create an acknowledgment jar where staff can share ways that their colleagues supported them. Choose a few to read at the start of meetings.
- Start a book club using *The Art of Self-Nurturing* to support others in prioritizing nurturing themselves.

- Have staff share how they have nurtured themselves and the difference it made on their work.
- Ask people to join you for a walk, bike ride, or to play a sport at lunch.
- Start a CSA (community-supported agriculture) at your work, so people have access to fresh, healthy food.
- Create more nurturing team-building opportunities, including holding a Health, Wellness, and Self-Nurturing Day at your office.
- Encourage your employer to offer telecommuting, if possible.
- Hold online forums to nurture community building.

Reflective
Questions

1.

WHAT NURTURING PRACTICES WOULD YOU LIKE
TO INTEGRATE AT WORK?

2.

WHO AT WORK COULD SUPPORT YOU IN CREATING
A CULTURE OF SELF-NURTURING?

3.

WHAT STEPS WOULD YOU NEED TO TAKE TO BRING
ONE OF THESE SELF-NURTURING PRACTICES TO
YOUR PLACE OF EMPLOYMENT?

4.

WHAT DIFFERENCE DO YOU THINK THIS
NURTURING PRACTICE WILL MAKE TO YOUR
ORGANIZATION?

Acknowledgements

My heart is overflowing with deep gratitude for so many people who have loved, encouraged, and supported me over the years to make the writing of this book possible.

As such, there are way too many individuals to name. Please know that my love and appreciation for every one of you are woven through these pages, and I am so grateful that you have been my village.

I want to thank my amazing husband, Tony, who has, for decades, loved, supported, and nurtured me like no other and has helped me manifest so much beauty and joy in my life.

I want to thank my darling daughters, Fiona and Zoey, who continue to teach me daily how essential it is to nurture and love myself and inspire me to share my passion with the world.

A special thanks to Zoey, who listened to my reading of the book out loud during the editing process and provided beautiful feedback.

I want to thank all of my family and friends who believed in me and held a vision of what was possible for me before I was ready to step into that space.

A special thanks to my sweet mom, who always encouraged my writing, my inspiring sister Karen, who has nurtured and supported me throughout my life, and my best friend Kelly, who has loved me unconditionally and inspires me to the best version of myself.

Thank you to all of my clients throughout the years who have trusted me to walk their healing journey with them and taught me how transformational self-nurturing could be.

A special thank you to my beloved mediation sangha, my inspiring Divas singing group, my darling book sisters book club, my remarkable colleagues and graduates at Leap to Success, and my beautiful soul sisters: all of you have inspired me to live authentically and courageously, and radiate peace, joy, love, gratitude, and compassion in the world!

Thank you to:

Deborah Kevin for your masterful editing of the book;

Rachel Dunham for allowing me to participate in the creative process resulting in this gorgeous book cover and beautiful interior layout and design; and

Linda Joy, my dear friend, and inspiring publisher, who has been waiting for years for me to write this book. Thank you for believing in me and the power of self-nurturing and mid-wifing this book into existence.

My profound gratitude for all who have loved me, taught me, encouraged me, challenged me, supported me, helped me grow, and believed in me.

May you know how much I love and cherish you!

About The Author

Kelley Grimes, MSW

Kelley Grimes, MSW, is an empowering counselor, self-nurturing expert, sought-after speaker, best-selling author, an expert columnist for Aspire Magazine, and an expert instructor for InspiredLivingUniversity.com. She is the founder of Cultivating Peace and Joy, inspiring individuals to nurture peace in the world from the inside out.

Kelley is passionate about empowering overwhelmed and exhausted individuals to live with more peace, joy, and meaning through the practice of self-nurturing. She loves working with individuals, couples, and families in person and virtually to transform their lives.

In addition, she provides professional and leadership development to organizations dedicated to making the world a better place. As a dynamic keynote and workshop presenter, she has been invited to present at these inspiring organizations: Alliance For Regional Solutions, Carlsbad Village Yoga, The Epilepsy Foundation, Exodus Recovery

Inc., Girls Rising, Hands of Peace, MAAC, Nordson Corporation, Regional Center, ResCare, Vista Community Clinic, and hospitals, community colleges, universities, and school districts throughout San Diego County on a variety of topics including self-nurturing, stress management, mindfulness, trauma-informed care, cultivating resilience, motivational interviewing, avoiding burnout, and staying grounded in uncertain times.

She teaches self-nurturing practices and strategies to women overcoming domestic violence, homelessness, and other major life challenges for Leap to Success, where she serves as the Director of Community Engagement, instructor, and leadership coach. Kelley is also a field instructor for San Diego State University, where she loves supervising and mentoring Masters of Social Work interns.

She is honored to have been awarded the Graduate "Above and Beyond" Field Instructor Award from San Diego State University and the "Olive Branch" Award from Hands of Peace.

Kelley lives in Carlsbad, California, and is married to an artist and board game maker, has two empowered and inspiring daughters, and loves singing with a small women's group. Learn more at www.cultivatingpeaceandjoy.com.

About The Publisher

Founded in 2010 by Inspirista, Sacred Visibility Catalyst, Mindset Mojo Mentor™, radio show host, and *Aspire Magazine* Publisher Linda Joy, Inspired Living Publishing, LLC. (ILP), is an international best-selling inspirational boutique hybrid publishing company. ILP is dedicated to publishing books for women and by women and spreading a message of love, positivity, feminine wisdom, and self-empowerment to women of all ages, backgrounds, and life paths. Linda's multimedia brands reach over 44,000 subscribers and a social media community of over 24,000 women.

Inspired Living Publishing works with mission-driven female entrepreneurs—heart-centered, mission-driven, coaches, therapists, service providers, and health practitioners in the personal and spiritual development genres, to bring their message and mission to life and to the world. ILP publishes, markets and launches select manuscripts by visionary female authors whose messages are aligned with ILP's philosophy of inspiration, authenticity, empowerment, and personal transformation.

Best-selling releases include *Everything Is Going to Be Okay: From the Projects to Harvard to Freedom* by Dr. Catherine Hayes, CPCC; *Awakening to Life: Your Sacred Guide to Consciously Creating a Life of Purpose, Magic, and Miracles* by Patricia Young; the award-winning *Being Love: How Loving Yourself Creates Ripples of Transformation in Your Relationships and the World* and *Soul-Hearted Living™: A Year of Sacred Reflections & Affirmations for Women* by Dr. Debra L. Reble; and the multiple award-winning *The Art of Inspiration: An Editor's Guide to Writing Powerful, Effective Inspirational & Personal Development Books,* by Bryna Haynes.

Through Inspired Living Publishing's highly successful sacred anthology division, ILP has brought multiple transformational books to bestseller status and provided over 300 visionary female authors an opportunity to share their story through the power of Authentic Storytelling™.

What sets Inspired Living Publishing™ apart is the powerful, high-visibility publishing, marketing, bestseller launch, and exposure across multiple media platforms that are included in our packages. ILP's family of authors reap the benefits of being a part of a sacred family of inspirational multimedia brands that deliver the best in transformational and empowering content across a wide range of platforms.

Our hybrid publishing packages and à la carte marketing and media packages provide transformational authors with access to our proven bestseller model and high-profile multimedia exposure across all of Linda's imprints (including *Aspire Magazine,* the "Inspired Conversations" radio show on OMTimes Radio, the Inspired Living Giveaway, Inspired

Living Secrets, and exposure to Linda's loyal personal audience of over 44,000 women.)

If you're ready to publish your transformational book or share your story in one of ours, we invite you to join us! Learn more about our publishing services at **InspiredLiving-Publishing.com.**

INSPIRED LIVING PUBLISHING ~ TRANSFORMING WOMEN'S LIVES, ONE STORY AT A TIME™

If you enjoyed this book, visit
www.InspiredLivingPublishing.com
and sign up for ILP's e-zine to receive news about
hot new releases, promotions, and information on
exciting author events.

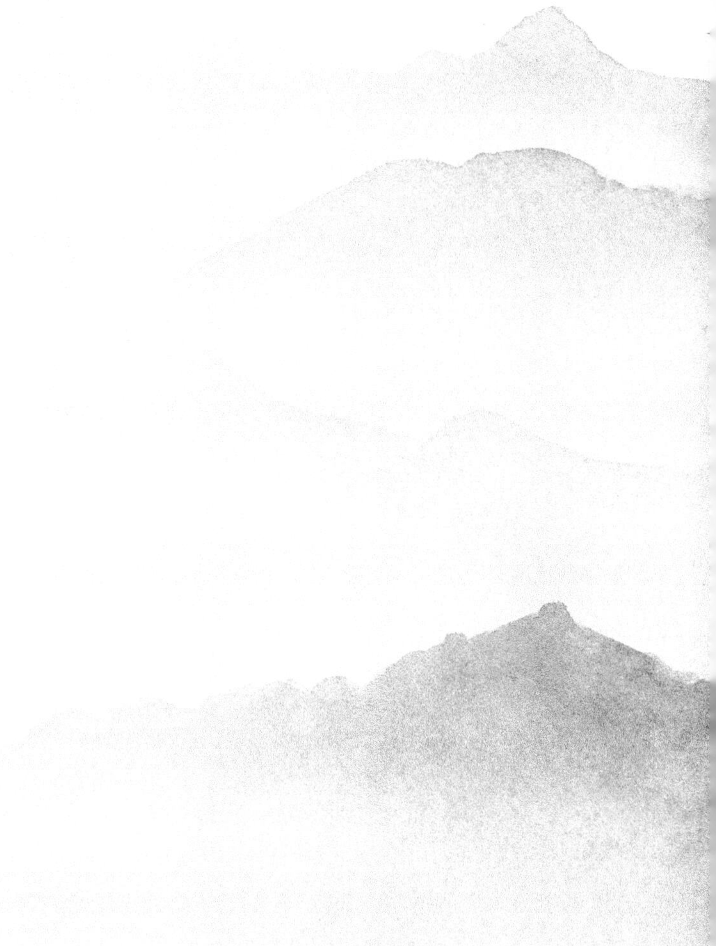

CPSIA information can be obtained
at www.ICGtesting.com
Printed in the USA
BVHW051243040322
630605BV00005B/14